Recipes
FROM A
Wisconsin Inn

Recipes
FROM A
Wisconsin Inn
✿ Lynn Greene

Happiness is a busy Kitchen — Enjoy!

Lynn Greene

COUNTRY ROADS PRESS
Oaks • Pennsylvania

Recipes from a Wisconsin Inn
© 1996 by Lynn Greene. All rights reserved.
Published by Country Roads Press
P.O. Box 838, 2170 West Drive
Oaks, PA 19456

Cover & text illustrations by Lois Leonard Stock.
Text design & typesetting by Allen Crider.

ISBN 1-56626-143-0

Printed in the United States of America.
10 9 8 7 6 5 4 3 2 1

Library of Congress Cataloguing-in-Publication Data

Greene, Lynn,
        Recipes from a Wisconsin inn / Lynn Greene.
            p.   cm.
        Includes index.
        ISBN 1-56626-143-0
        1. Greene House Country Inn (Whitewater, Wis.)   2. Cookery, American.   I. Title.
        TX715.G81195   1995
        641.5'09775'89--dc20   95-18378
                                                                            CIP

RECIPES FROM A WISCONSIN INN

By: Lynn Greene
The Greene House Country Inn, Highway 12, West #5666
Whitewater, Wisconsin, 53190-9412 (414-495-8771)

This book is dedicated to all of those parents, grandparents, sisters
and brothers, friends and relatives who have taught the love of cooking to those of the next generation.

Contents

1 **Green Eggs and Ham** 1
Green Eggs and Ham 3
Crêpes with Fresh Peaches 4
Country Scramble 6
Oatmeal Pancakes 7
Butter Biscuits with Apple Butter .8
Cranberry Bread Pudding 9

2 **Aphrodisiacs for Two, Valentine's Day Dinner** 11
Baked Brie with Garlic Crust 13
Broiled Oysters on the Half Shell 14
Steamed Artichokes with Honey Butter 15
Chocolate Raspberry Cheesecake 16

3 **Take a Walk on the Wild Side** 19
Spring Greens Salad with Raspberry Vinaigrette 21
Beer Batter Fiddleheads 22
Wild Rice Sauté 23
Morel Sauté 24
Black Walnut Pie 25

4 **Garden Club Luncheon** 27
Garden Salad with Citrus Dressing 29
Broccoli and Ham Quiche 30
Lion-naise Potatoes 32
Rhubarb Torte 33
Chamomile-and-Mint Iced Tea 34

5 **Old World Wisconsin** 35
Yankee Pot Roast 37
Pierogi 38
Irish Soda Bread 40
Blueberry Blintzes 42

6   **Great Lakes Fish Fry** 45
Pan Fried Bluegills, Tartar Sauce 47
Crunchy Coleslaw 48
Potato Pancakes 49
Homemade Ice Cream with Mocha Fudge Sauce 50

7   **Bluegrass Picnic** 53
Whole Wheat Bread 55
Homemade Chicken Salad 56
Vegetarian Sandwich Filling 57
Perfect Potato Salad 58
Roman Apple Cake 59

8   **Puttin' on the Grill** 61
Hot Spinach and Bacon Salad 62
Grilled Smoked Turkey Breast with Basting Sauces 63
Vegetable Kabobs 65
Caramelized Fruit over Baked Custard 66

9   **Farmers' Market Buffet** 67
Cabbage Patch Soup 69
Farmers' Market Salad 70
Freezer-Batter Zucchini Bread 71
Apple Tart 72

10   **Jammin' Time** 73
Strawberry Sauce 75
Sugarless Strawberry Jam 75
Cranberry Cherry Sauce 77
Apple Jam 78
Orange Marmalade 79

11   **County Fair Favorites** 81
Cinnamon Rolls 83
Church Tent Fried Chicken 84
Chuck Wagon Chili 85
Sweet Adelines Cream Puffs 86

12   **The Great Cookie Bakeoff** 87

Gingerbread Cookie Cutouts 89

Fruit Cake Gems 90

Rum Balls 91

A Gingerbread House Of Your Own 92

Cooked Eggnog 96

13   **A German Christmas** 97

Roast Pheasant with Dressing 99

Spätzle 100

Stollen 101

14   **Ski Weekend** 103

Chicken Soup with Kreplach 105

Brewery Black Bean Soup 107

Mom's Best Oatmeal Bread 108

Pumpkin Bread 109

15   **Miscellany** 111

Herbal Blend for No-Salt Diets 113

Ragin' Cajun 114

Italian Seasoning 115

Horehound Cough Drops 116

Cold Deterrent 117

Candied Violets 118

Herbal Vinegars 119

Dog Gone Biscuits 120

A Cook's Favorite Bird Food Recipe 121

Replacement Formula 122

Introduction

It is wonderful to be able to do what you want. And that is exactly what Mayner and Lynn Greene are doing.

Mayner indulges his love of guitars by placing them everywhere in the Greene House Country Inn. Literally. Dining room, bathrooms, guestrooms—each room has its collection of stringed instruments. As a guest, you may play them or simply listen to them being played.

Lynn, for her part, has a love affair with the country; with old farm houses, with the animals of the countryside, and with everyday country eating.

Lynn cooks simple but imaginative food that both fills the stomach and feeds the soul. A garden of flavors lies just outside her door.

And ethnic variety is part and parcel of her cooking. German and Polish, English and Irish, those are her roots. But her cooking experience also includes such international specialties as kreplach and blintzes.

Here, too, are both the familiar and the unexpected: Brewery Black Bean Soup and Broiled Oysters on the Shell, suggestions for a no-salt herbal spice blend, and a full menu to cook on the grill.

The Greene House Country Inn has given Lynn a place to indulge in cooking, not just cook; a place to satisfy customers, not just cook satisfactorily.

Whether your taste runs to Green Eggs and Ham or a Friday-night fish fry, you are bound to enjoy the food at this place in the country.

Chapter One

Green Eggs and Ham

Breakfast is the most important meal of the day. Surely, you have heard that before. And at the Greene House Country Inn, breakfast is one of the most important things we do for our guests.

You could start your day here with any number of specialties, but the one item that always captures the imagination is the Green Eggs and Ham. Being a Dr. Seuss fan from way back, I love to make this entrée.

Playing on our last name of Greene, we have filled our backyard barn with araucanas, chickens that lay green eggs. For some reason, my younger guests accept this information quite as fact and immediately ask to see the eggs. Whereas my older guests usually just look at me. Sort of funny. Sometimes we do grow up too quickly.

My own version of this favorite Seussism is made with a spinach-and-cheese sauce. You could serve it for any meal and receive rave reviews.

All breakfasts served at our Inn are hearty. Given that most guests come to enjoy all the outdoor activities available, this feature is much appreciated.

Crêpes with Fresh Peaches

Country Scramble

Oatmeal Pancakes

*Butter Biscuits with
    Apple Butter*

Cranberry Bread Pudding

In addition, many Country Inn guests are very involved in health and environmental issues. Organic ingredients may be a strong preference for some. And it is an unusual week indeed that we don't see at least a few vegetarians gathered at the breakfast table.

At the Greene House Country Inn we accommodate these concerns by using only fresh ingredients, locally grown if possible.

Our own large garden will serve up many of the vegetables, fruits, and salad greens used in the meals we serve. We do not use pesticides or sprays of any kind.

And those chickens we were talking about? Special chickens such as these range freely, of course, and are fed an organic diet, free of chemicals.

Just like our house guests.

Please remember that when those roosters wake you up in the morning.

Green Eggs and Ham

Serves 6

---

6 English muffins

12 eggs, beaten

6 tablespoons milk

2 tablespoons butter

6 slices of breakfast ham

Clean the spinach leaves, removing the tough stems. Chop coarse and steam or microwave until just tender. Meanwhile, make the sauce.

Drain the cooked spinach and add to sauce. Keep sauce warm. Split and toast English muffins. Mix the eggs and 6 tablespoons of milk together and cook in frying pan with 2 tablespoons butter, scrambling the eggs as they cook. Arrange the two halves of an English muffin on each plate and spoon the eggs evenly over the muffins. Cover with the spinach-and-cheese sauce. Serve with a side order of ham.

Sauce

1 pound fresh spinach leaves

½ cup butter or margarine

½ cup flour

3½ cups milk

1 cup grated Swiss cheese

⅛ teaspoon white pepper

¼ teaspoon salt (optional)

½ teaspoon hot sauce (optional)

In saucepan, melt the butter or margarine. Add the flour while whisking to form a roux. Cook for 1 minute to brown the flour slightly. Add milk while whisking, to form a smooth sauce. Add grated cheese and cook for 5 to 10 minutes, until cheese is incorporated and melted completely. Add pepper, salt, and hot sauce.

Crêpes with Fresh Peaches

Makes 8 to 10 shells, depending on pan size

Crêpe Shells

2 eggs

2 tablespoons oil

1 cup milk

I cup flour

dash salt

6"–8" frying pan (a nonstick omelet pan works great.)

In mixer bowl, beat eggs slightly with wire whisk. Add remaining ingredients and whisk together. Do not over-beat—there will still be small lumps of flour in the mixture and that's okay.

Preheat the pan. When a drop of water hisses and skitters in the pan, then evaporates, it is hot enough. Some pans will require a little oil; a spray product works well.

Pour the batter into the pan, using a ¼-cup measure for a 6" pan, a ⅓-cup measure for a larger pan. Immediately rotate and tilt the pan to get the mixture to cover the bottom evenly. Do this as close to the burner as possible to maintain the cooking.

Let the shell cook until lightly browned at the edges and starting to get dry. The shiny batter in the center will be the last to cook. Once the shine is gone, it is time to flip. Use a spatula or turner to loosen the edge all around, then position the spatula under the center of the shell and flip it over. It needs to cook on the second side for only a few seconds. Tip the pan to turn the shell out on a plate. Stack the shells as you make them, separating them with pieces of waxed paper.

To serve, spread ½ cup of filling on the crêpe shell in a line down the center. Fold the top edge over onto the filling. Complete the rolling process and place the crêpe seam side down on a serving plate. Serve with whipped cream.

Crêpes with Fresh Peaches, continued

Filling

8 to 10 fresh peaches, peeled and sliced

2 tablespoons butter

2 tablespoons maple syrup

½ teaspoon cinnamon

¼ teaspoon nutmeg

½ cup apricot jam or other fruit jam

In sauté pan, melt the butter. Add the peaches and cook while stirring until peaches are just tender. Add remaining ingredients and cook just until jam is completely melted and covers the peaches.

Country Scramble

Serves 4

2 pounds medium red potatoes

½ pound bacon

1 large Spanish onion

1 large green bell pepper

1 large red bell pepper

1 pound mushrooms, sliced thick

½ pound bulk breakfast sausage

1 teaspoon black pepper

1 teaspoon Hungarian paprika

salt to taste

6 eggs, beaten

4 slices American cheese (1 ounce each)

Clean potatoes but do not peel. Cover with water and boil until tender; drain and let cool. Meanwhile, chop the bacon, onions, and peppers into ½" pieces. Add to sauté pan along with mushrooms and sausage. Cook until bacon and sausage are done. (If there is not sufficient fat in the bacon and sausage to sauté the ingredients, add a few tablespoons of butter or margarine.)

Slice the cooked red potatoes ¼" thick and add to the pan along with pepper, paprika, and salt. Mix together. Pour the beaten eggs evenly over these ingredients and cook, covered, until eggs are done. They will be dry to the touch. Arrange the cheese slices on top and cook, covered, just until cheese has melted. Cut into quarters and serve.

Oatmeal Pancakes
Makes 6

¾ cup quick-cooking oatmeal

1 ½ cups buttermilk

1 large egg, slightly beaten

½ cup whole-wheat flour

½ teaspoon salt

½ teaspoon baking soda

1 tablespoon maple syrup

Pour buttermilk over oatmeal and let stand in refrigerator overnight. The next morning, add all other ingredients, mixing well. (This batter is a bit thicker than most, but you can thin it down with additional buttermilk if it seems too thick to pour.) Grease your griddle a bit or use a nonstick pan. Heat the griddle to 375° F. and pour batter to form 6 pancakes with room to spread. Cook over low heat. When bubbles start to form on the top side, it is time to turn the pancakes. Cook just until brown on the second side. Serve with warmed maple syrup.

Butter Biscuits
Makes 8

A really simple recipe with a melt-in-the-mouth texture.

⅔ cup butter

2 teaspoons salt

2 tablespoons sugar

2 tablespoons double-acting
    baking powder

3 cups flour

1½ cups warm milk (about 110°F.)

Make a crumb mixture of all ingredients except milk, using a pastry cutter. (A fork will work, too.) Add milk and stir together just until moistened. Do not overmix! Let batter rest 10 minutes. Using an ice-cream scoop, drop 8 large scoops on ungreased baking sheet. (A ¼-cup measure will work if you don't have a scoop; just be sure to compress the batter enough to keep it together for baking.) Bake 15 to 20 minutes in a 375° F. oven. Serve with apple butter.

Apple Butter
Makes 4 pints

3 pounds windfall apples*

3 quarts raw apple cider

1½ cups maple syrup

½ cup brown sugar

2 teaspoons cinnamon

½ teaspoon cloves

½ teaspoon mace (optional)

Wash, peel, and core apples and slice thinly. Place slices in a heavy stockpot and cover with apple cider. Cook for 1 hour. Press through a sieve or colander to produce pulp. Return the pulp to the stockpot and add remaining ingredients. Cook over low heat for 1 to 2 hours, stirring frequently to avoid scorching. Pour into 4 pint jars. Process in boiling-water bath or let cool and refrigerate.

*Windfall apples are tree-ripened (and thus flavorful) apples that have fallen to the ground. You may use any good baking apple.

Cranberry Bread Pudding

Serves 4

1½ cups milk

1 teaspoon grated lemon zest

dash of salt

¼ cup honey

2 large eggs, beaten

1 teaspoon vanilla extract

1 cup cranberries, coarsely chopped

1½ to 2 cups stale bread cubes

In mixer or by hand, beat together first six ingredients. Add cranberries and bread and mix together with spoon. Pour into a 1½-quart baking dish that has been lightly greased. Cover with aluminum foil and bake at 325° F. for 25 minutes. Test by inserting tip of knife in middle. If the knife comes out dry, the pudding is done. Serve warm with ice cream.

Chapter Two

Aphrodisiacs for Two

Saint Valentine's Day has been around for quite some time now, and there is no better way to celebrate "Just the Two of Us" than by having a quiet evening at home with a wonderful meal.

But, this day being what it is, something more is usually expected. So taking a look at all the ingredients believed at one time or another to be aphrodisiacs, we've come up with a wonderful menu for two.

You may be interested to know that Saint Valentine was a historical figure who lost his life for love. You see, he violated a ruling that stated no marriages were to be performed while a war was being fought. This was to ensure the nobility of plenty of unattached young warriors.

Bishop Valentine found the lovers' fate so disturbing that he continued to perform the rite in secret. After his death and down through history, Saint Valentine became a symbol of love eternal.

The background of the word "aphrodisiac" is no less complicated. It refers to Aphrodite, who was no mere mortal but a goddess who can still be seen today in many statues, carvings, and reliefs. At times, she is pictured with Eros (whence the word

Baked Brie with Garlic Crust

Broiled Oysters on the Half Shell

Steamed Artichokes with Honey Butter

Chocolate Raspberry Cheesecake

"erotica" came). Doves attend her, and she is partial to the rose and the lily. Her special fruit is the apple of fertility.

This beautiful Immortal is also known as the Goddess of Dawn, as she brought the light into the world each day. When we are in love, it is said that this same light or glow emanates from us. Aphrodite is guided by her passions and has lent her name down through history to those things that induce passion—aphrodisiacs.

All races and all cultures have embraced the idea that certain foods or potions will cause one to feel more passionate.

On our menu, garlic is from the Romans, who believed it to have an invigorating ability.

Early Americans may have scoffed at this ancient belief, but only because they were sure that the only true aphrodisiac was the oyster. Considering how plentiful oysters were in Colonial America and how quickly we took over the American continent through a sheer population explosion, we are willing to grant this shelled delicacy the benefit of the doubt.

In Elizabethan England, on the other hand, doctors prescribed artichokes to pump up performance. They even went so far as to use this vegetable's name as slang for a woman with a questionable occupation.

And then we have chocolate. Actually, this ingredient can be credited to Montezuma, who has a lot of followers in his choice of stimulant. The Aztec emperor was reputed to drink his version of the chocolate phosphate before visiting his very large harem. We know now that chocolate contains caffeine, so we can assume that at least Montezuma stayed awake.

Baked Brie With Garlic Crust

Serves 2

A 12-ounce round of Brie cheese

3 sheets of phyllo dough

4 tablespoons butter

6 cloves garlic, crushed

¼ teaspoon marjoram

¼ teaspoon black pepper, freshly ground

Chill the cheese. Melt butter and add the crushed garlic. Sauté for one minute. Remove three sheets of phyllo dough from the package and lay each separately on the counter. Brush each sheet of phyllo dough with the garlic butter. Lay the cheese round in the center of one sheet of dough and fold the dough around it, turning the cheese until the entire sheet is used. Continue with the second and third sheet to encase the cheese completely. Place the wrapped cheese on a baking sheet and bake in a preheated 400° F. oven for 15 minutes or until the pastry turns a golden color and is crisp to the touch. Remove from oven and serve immediately with crackers or toasted bread squares.

Broiled Oysters On the Half Shell
Serves 2

2 dozen fresh oysters in their shells

1 fresh lemon

2 tablespoons butter

3 tablespoons onion, chopped fine

3 tablespoons bacon, cooked and chopped
   fine (optional)

1 cup dry bread crumbs, ground fine

1 teaspoon parsley

dash of salt (optional)

1 egg, beaten with 2 tablespoons water

Shuck oysters, saving one half of each shell. Squeeze lemon over the oysters and let marinate. Meanwhile, in a sauté pan, melt butter and add the onion and bacon. Sauté onion until tender. Remove from heat and add bread crumbs, parsley, and salt. Dip each oyster in the beaten-egg mixture, then in the crumb mixture. Place one oyster in each of the shells. Broil in a preheated oven for 5 to 10 minutes, until oysters are cooked through. The time will depend on the thickness of the oysters and the temperature of your broiler. Remove and serve each portion on a large platter with cocktail sauce and additional lemon.

Cocktail Sauce

½ cup catsup

2 teaspoons lemon juice, freshly squeezed

2 teaspoons horseradish, freshly grated

1 teaspoon Worcestershire sauce

Combine all ingredients. The sauce may be kept refrigerated for up to a week.

Steamed Artichokes

Serves 2

2 whole artichokes

1 tablespoon lemon juice

1 clove garlic

Whole artichokes can be found in most good produce sections. To prepare these globes for cooking, wash them thoroughly by dunking in a bowl of water several times. Next, trim the tip of each leaf with your kitchen shears to remove the tiny barbs you won't want to contend with once your dining experience begins.

Cut the bottoms of the artichokes flat so they have secure bases to stand on. Now stand the artichokes upright in a pan containing 1 to 2 inches of water, the lemon juice, and the garlic. (Artichoke "racks" in gourmet kitchen stores are designed to hold the vegetables upright while cooking—nice, but not necessary.) Bring to a boil and steam with the cover on for 45 minutes. Drain and serve with honey butter.

To eat: Using your fingers, remove a leaf by pulling it gently toward you. Dip the base of the leaf in the honey butter and run through the teeth to extract the pulpy "meat." Discard fibrous remains of leaf. Continue eating a leaf at a time until you get down to the lighter-colored cone in the middle. With a knife, cut away the fuzzy center at the base; eat the remaining heart with a fork.

Honey Butter

½ cup butter, softened

¼ cup honey

Combine. Serve at room temperature or melt in a microwave oven set on low for 1 minute.

Chocolate Raspberry Cheesecake

32 ounces cream cheese, softened

5 whole eggs

1 cup granulated sugar

1 cup sour cream

1 teaspoon vanilla extract

1 pint whipping cream (or half and half)

½ cup flour

6 ounces bittersweet chocolate

2 tablespoons butter

¾ cup raspberry preserves

In mixer bowl, beat the cream cheese until smooth. Add the eggs and granulated sugar. Beat well. Add sour cream and vanilla extract. Beat well. Add whipping cream and beat well. Add flour and beat well. Divide batter in half. Place the bittersweet chocolate and butter in a microwavable bowl and microwave on low for 30 seconds. If chocolate has not melted, heat a little more, but do not continue once it is melted. Add this chocolate mixture to first half of batter and blend. To second half of batter, add the raspberry preserves and blend well. Pour one-half of chocolate mixture into prepared crust. Top with one half of raspberry mixture, then remaining chocolate mixture, then remaining raspberry mixture. Swirl all the layers together with a butter knife. Do not overmix at this point. Place on baking sheet and bake in a preheated 350° F. oven for 15 minutes. Reduce heat to 250° F. and continue baking for 1 hour. Remove from oven and run knife around edge of pan to loosen cheesecake. Turn off oven and return cheesecake to oven for 30 minutes. Serve warm or chill thoroughly and serve with a dollop of whipped cream.

Crust

½ cup butter or margarine

¾ cup flour

¼ cup granulated sugar

¼ cup almonds, ground fine

½ teaspoon almond extract (or vanilla)

In bowl, cut the flour and sugar into butter to form a crumbly mixture. Add almonds and mix together with your hands. In a lightly greased 12" springform pan, press the crust into place, bringing it up the edges just slightly. Bake in preheated 350° F. oven for 10 minutes before filling with cheesecake batter.

Chapter Three

Take a Walk on the Wild Side

Spring comes to Wisconsin. Really. But that is about all you can count on, since you don't really know when it will come or if what you think is spring is for real or just teasing you. Sometimes you can be out planting your garden, thinking that this is finally the year you will be ahead of the game. And then it will start to snow.

So, it is inevitable that when spring finally arrives, the fever has already been swirling around in your blood for some time. That's when you really have to get out and take a walk on the wild side!

Outdoors is where you need to be—tramping across field and stream, into the forest and pine woods, under the canopy of oak and ash trees.

A hop, skip, and a jump away is the Kettle Moraine Forest with hundreds of miles of trails. Hikers, mountain bikers, and horseback riders all enjoy their own paths. So go on, get out there.

But make sure you take a basket and a pocket knife. These are really the only two essentials you will need to collect a wild harvest of your own. And spring is definitely the time to do it.

Spring Greens Salad with Raspberry Vinaigrette

Beer Batter Fiddleheads

Wild Rice Sauté

Morel Saute

Black Walnut Pie

The morels start to pop their heads above ground, just a little, then, oomph, they make one last push and their blanket of oak leaves is turned aside. It's as if they beg you to find them. If you know your wild mushrooms or have a friend along who is knowledgeable, then you've found dinner—but do be sure you know what you're picking! And a delicious dinner it is. They taste so good (nothing like those plebeian mushrooms you find in the store) and the best way to prepare them is the simplest.

While you're out there with your basket, keep your eyes open for fiddleheads. No, they are not some silly musicians wandering around in the woods, but the first growth of cinnamon, ostrich, or bracken ferns. The emerging, coiled greenery is the same shape as the head of a fiddle. Covered in a simple beer batter and fried, they are quite tasty.

But spring really means … green. And spring greens are the best, high in vitamins, too. Just the thing for a jump start into healthier summertime eating. The good thing about greens is that if they taste edible, they usually are. (Remember you do have to be more careful with wild mushrooms.)

Let's see, a bowl of fresh spring greens to start off the meal. Then a tasty appetizer of fiddleheads, followed by a hearty main course of Wild Rice Sauté, with a side dish of morels. Top it off with a nice black-walnut pie. Now that's a meal worth shopping for. See you in the woods.

Spring Greens with Raspberry Vinaigrette

Serves 6

1 bunch* dandelion greens

1 bunch* watercress

1 bunch* lamb's quarters

1 bunch* poke weed

1 bunch* mustard greens

½ cup craisons (dried cranberries)

½ cup sunflower seeds

Wash all greens thoroughly and let dry in a colander or pat dry with paper towel. Place in a large bowl and add craisons and sunflower seeds. Pour dressing over entire contents and toss.

Raspberry Vinaigrette

½ cup raspberry vinegar

¼ cup sunflower oil

3 tablespoons honey

1 tablespoon garlic, freshly crushed

Combine all ingredients and whisk together until well blended.

*About 1 to 1½ cups, for each of the greens.

Beer-Batter Fiddleheads

Serves 4-6 (Enough to coat 1 pound cleaned fiddleheads)

1½ cups flour

1 teaspoon salt (optional)

¼ teaspoon ground white pepper

2 tablespoons salad oil

2 eggs, beaten

¾ cup flat beer (can be stale or open
      and let sit to "flatten")

½ inch of oil in frying pan, heated to 365° F.

Mix all batter ingredients together. Let rest in refrigerator for several hours or at room temperature for about 20 minutes. Pat fiddleheads dry with toweling and dredge in batter. Immediately place in hot oil in frying pan and fry on each side about 2 minutes or until lightly browned. Remove and drain. Keep warm in low oven, uncovered, until all are cooked. Serve with cocktail sauce or horseradish sauce if desired.

Horseradish Sauce

Makes 2½ cups

1 piece horseradish root

1 pair of rubber gloves

1 set of goggles

1 pint whipping cream

½ cup mayonnaise

¼ teaspoon ground mustard

1 teaspoon sugar

¼ teaspoon salt

⅛ teaspoon white pepper

Using the rubber gloves and the eye goggles to protect yourself, peel the horseradish root and grate it, using the finest holes on your grater. Retain the grated horseradish and the juice. You will need about ¼ cup grated horseradish to complete the recipe. Combine all remaining ingredients and whisk together. Add horseradish and stir in. Keep covered. The sauce will keep for up to two weeks in the refrigerator.

Wild Rice Sauté

Serves 6 - 8

---

4 tablespoons margarine

2 pounds venison, cut in ½" cubes*

¾ cup wild rice

¾ cup brown rice

2 apples, peeled and diced

½ cup pecans, chopped coarse

1 teaspoon dried chopped parsley

½ teaspoon dried thyme

3 cups chicken stock or water

In cooking pot with lid, melt margarine. Add the cubed venison and sauté until just cooked through. Add wild and brown rice, apples, and pecans. Sauté these ingredients over low heat until apples soften slightly. Add parsley, thyme, and chicken stock or water. Bring to a boil. Stir, then cover with lid. Turn down heat to a low simmer and cook 15 to 20 minutes more or until rice is done. (Wild rice can vary in cooking time required). Stir once just before rice is fully cooked to incorporate ingredients, as they tend to separate during cooking process.

*Venison may be omitted. Or you may substitute almost any other type of meat: beef, pork, chicken, turkey, or duck.

Morel Sauté

1 pound morel mushrooms

4 tablespoons butter

2 tablespoons green onions, chopped fine

½ teaspoon dried thyme, crushed

dash of salt (optional)

dash of ground white pepper

1 tablespoon Worcestershire sauce

Slice the morels lengthwise and wash to remove any dirt from the pockets. Pat dry on toweling. Place all ingredients except Worcestershire sauce in sauté pan and sauté slowly over medium heat until morels are tender and onions become translucent. Add Worcestershire sauce, toss, and serve with garlic toast.

Black Walnut Pie
Serves 8

1 single-shell 9" pie crust (recipe follows)

2 tablespoons margarine

3 eggs

1 cup maple syrup

⅓ cup brown sugar

1 teaspoon vanilla

1½ cups black walnuts, shelled and halved

Melt the margarine in a saucepan. Let cool slightly, then add eggs and beat well. Add syrup, sugar, and vanilla and beat well. Pour this mixture into prepared pie crust. Sprinkle the walnuts evenly on top. Bake at 350° F. for 50 minutes or until a knife inserted in middle of pie comes out clean.

"Simple as Pie" Crust
Makes one double crust or two single crusts.

This recipe is hard to work with if cut in half; instead make two single crusts and freeze the second one.

1 cup flour

½ cup shortening or margarine

4 tablespoons water, ice cold

Put flour in bowl and cut in shortening with pastry cutter. Add the water and stir until a ball of dough is formed. Add more water if necessary (some flours, at certain times of the year, absorb more liquid.) Flour your counter and turn out dough. Knead quickly, just to form a pliable single ball. Cover and let rest in refrigerator for at least 15 minutes. Divide dough in half and roll out each half to a circle about 12" in diameter. Lightly grease and flour a 9" pie plate. Line pie plate with dough and flute edges with fingers or fold ends over neatly and mark with fork tines for a decorative edging.

Chapter Four

Garden Club Luncheon

Aaahh, the pleasures of a summertime garden. There is nothing quite like it. Working out in the garden on a quiet summer morning, with the sun warming you, maybe the dog or cat for company—that's the good life.

The old joke is that Wisconsin folks judge you by only two things: the size of your woodpile and the intensity of your garden.

A well-stocked wood pile would lead others to think that you are an industrious soul—thinking ahead, protecting your family from the ravages of winter, be it ever so far from your mind at the moment.

And a garden, well, a nicely laid-out plot shows a planner, an engineer. If every row is marked with the variety and date planted, that shows a compulsive type—or a seed saver.

I'm not sure what people think of my garden space. It's just as likely to have flowers as vegetables. When I'm out there working, I'm likely to take along a friend or two; even the geese will help out occasionally. And if a dog digs a hole, why, I guess that's as good a spot as any to start planting those seed potatoes.

As for a nice grid of tall things here, short ones there—you won't find that either. First of all, you have to adjust for the vol-

*Garden Salad with
    Citrus Dressing*

Broccoli and Ham Quiche

Lion-naise Potatoes

Rhubarb Torte

*Chamomile-and-Mint
    Iced Tea*

27

unteers, those plants that come up on their own in the spring. I just work around them, figuring that if they hid out all winter just to poke their heads up to say "Hi," I'd better treat them with some respect.

Companion planting is what I like to do. If carrots love tomatoes, then that is where they should be. And you will never see one of those tomatoes without a friendly marigold plant or two watching over it.

Then there are those crops that I never get to see on my dinner table, but I do get to see wonderful creatures making them their dinner. Spring green beans for the deer, tender spinach for the rabbits, and sunflower heads that bob in the wind as the birds try to catch a loose seed.

So a garden is both a place to be and a place to be seen. And a garden-club luncheon is the opportunity to display your gardening prowess. Around here you might even say it has become a highly competitive event. The object is to use the largest number of ingredients from your garden in one meal.

That is the purpose of our Garden Club Luncheon.

Garden Salad with Citrus Dressing

Serves 6

1½ cups Bibb lettuce

1½ cups red leaf lettuce

1½ cups endive

1 cup fresh asparagus, cut into 1" lengths

¾ cup fresh strawberries, sliced

¾ cup fresh or frozen blueberries

1 yellow tomato

1 red tomato

1 orange

1 lemon

1 lime

3 tablespoons olive oil

3 tablespoons honey

Wash and clean the lettuces and endive, removing tough stems. Cut greens into 3" pieces. Let drain or pat dry with paper toweling. Steam or microwave asparagus until just tender. Drain and chill. In large bowl combine lettuces, endive, asparagus, strawberries, and blueberries. Cut the tomatoes into 1" cubes and add to bowl. In a smaller bowl, squeeze the juice of the orange, lemon, and lime, straining out the seeds. Whisk in the olive oil and honey until combined well. Pour this dressing over the salad mixture and toss. Serve well chilled.

Broccoli and Ham Quiche

Serves 4–6

1 prepared single pie crust, 9" or 10" deep-dish size

½ pound fresh broccoli florets

1 tablespoon butter

¼ cup onions, chopped fine

½ pound ham

4 ounces mozzarella cheese, shredded

4 ounces Swiss cheese, shredded

4 eggs

1¾ cups half and half

dash of salt (optional)

⅛ teaspoon nutmeg

⅛ teaspoon white pepper

1 tablespoon fresh parsley, chopped, or one teaspoon dried

Wash broccoli and chop into ½" chunks. Steam or microwave until just tender. In large sauté pan, melt butter. Add onions and sauté until translucent. Cut ham into ½" chunks. In the same sauté pan, mix the onions with broccoli, ham, and cheeses. Spread the mixture evenly in prepared crust. In separate bowl, beat eggs until just frothy. Add half and half, salt, nutmeg, white pepper, and parsley and mix. Pour this mixture over the ingredients in the shell. Place quiche on baking sheet to catch any drips as it bakes. Bake in preheated 375° F. oven for 45 minutes to 1 hour, until a knife inserted in the middle comes out clean. Quiche should be served at a very warm temperature for the best flavor. Let it rest for just 15 minutes, then cut into 4 or 6 pieces and serve.

The Story of the Tiger Lilies

When we bought this old house in 1985, it had seen better days. One of the first things I wanted to do was get some flower beds going. But when you need a roof and water heaters, porches and siding, there isn't much left in the budget for flower beds.

So I took to eyeballing everyone else's garden and started begging for perennial divisions to help get me started. Visiting my brother Bob one day, I spied a pile of tiger lilies. "Hey, what you doing with those—planting them?" I asked.

"Heck no," he yelled, "I'm burning the ?*%$ things!" Turns out, they had dug their claws in all over his yard, playing havoc with his garden grid. (He's one of those.)

"I'll take them," I said, thinking the lilies would be just the thing to cover those empty spots on the front walkway. And they were free.

Ten years later, I'm ready to burn them. They have leaped over the walk and made themselves at home on the other side. They've gotten so aggressive I nearly expect guests to sport claw marks on their ankles after maneuvering through them.

But life offers all kinds of hidden rewards: I discovered that tiger-lily tubers not only are quite edible, but are also quite tasty. Tender young ones are the best.

꘎꘎꘎

Lion-Naise Potatoes

Serves 4 ferocious appetites

6–8 red potatoes, medium size

3 tablespoons butter

3 tablespoons margarine

1 medium onion

½ cup cleaned, sliced tiger-lily tubers

2 tablespoon fresh chives, chopped

dash of salt (optional)

½ teaspoon Hungarian paprika

¼ teaspoon white pepper

Wash but do not peel potatoes. Boil until tender. Drain. In large sauté pan, melt butter and margarine. Chop onion into ½" pieces and add to pan, along with the sliced tiger-lily tubers. Sauté until onions are translucent and golden. Add potatoes and sauté to an even brown. Add seasonings and serve, garnished with a tiger-lily bloom.

Rhubarb Torte

Serves 12

6 cups of fresh rhubarb, cleaned,*
    cut in ½" pieces

6 cups boiling water

1 cup sugar

1 cup brown sugar

½ cup flour

3 whole eggs, beaten

1 tablespoon vanilla

2 cups streusel

1 cup fresh raspberries**

Lightly grease and flour a 9" springform pan. Prepare streusel (recipe follows). Pour 4 cups of boiling water over the rhubarb and let stand for 30 minutes. Drain. To the rhubarb add the sugar, flour, eggs, and vanilla and mix. Pat 1 cup of streusel firmly into springform pan, bringing it slightly up the sides. Pour rhubarb mixture into the pan. Top with 1 cup of raspberries and sprinkle remaining cup of streusel evenly over the raspberries. Pat down gently to firm it and even the top. Bake in a 350° F. oven for 1 hour. Serve warm with ice cream.

Streusel Topping

Makes 2 cups

¾ cup flour

½ cup sugar

¼ cup butter

½ cup margarine

½ cup quick-cooking oatmeal

In mixing bowl combine flour and sugar. Cut in butter and margarine with pastry cutter or fork to make a crumbly mixture. Add oatmeal and cut in. Will keep if stored in airtight bag in freezer.

*Please note that when you clean the rhubarb you should discard the leaves carefully, since they contain oxalic acid and can be poisonous to animals. Your best bet is to compost them.

**You may substitute fresh sliced strawberries. Or use either type of frozen fruit that has been thawed first, draining excess juice.

Chamomile-and-Mint Iced Tea

Makes ½ gallon

1 cup chamomile flowers

1 cup mint leaves, peppermint or spearmint

6 cups boiling water

1 lemon

¼ cup honey

3 cups ice cubes

Wash chamomile and mint. Place in bowl and pour boiling water over leaves. Let steep for 15 to 30 minutes. Strain, discarding leaves. To the tea, add the juice of the lemon and the honey. Whisk until well blended. Serve well iced, garnished with wedges of lemon and mint leaves.

Chapter Five

Old World Wisconsin

isconsin, like many of our states, shows an amalgamation of ethnic backgrounds. The earliest nineteenth-century settlers were mainly Yankees, New Englanders of English ancestry. My grandmother was a Taylor, a fine, upstanding (and very plentiful) name in our section of Walworth County. That means boiled dinners, pot roast, and Yankee ingenuity for using what you have. As a kid, during chicken-butchering time, I distinctly remember seeing my grandmother retrieve chicken feet for making gelatin.

My other grandmother was German, married to a Pole. Quite the combination! But the food was unbelievable. Grandma taught me how to make *pierogi*. And, hardworking German that she was, she made me feel guilty about everything I didn't get done.

There are many Danish and Norwegian Americans populating the southeast corner of Wisconsin as well. Kringle made in Racine is shipped all over the world.

Ethnic cooking, I've found, is best conducted with an adventurous spirit and an ability to make substitutions. Many cooks don't want to use lard in pie crust anymore—what with cholesterol figures that follow you around—even though lard

Yankee Pot Roast

Pierogi

Irish Soda Bread

Blueberry Blintzes

traditionally makes the best crust. And don't worry, there are no ingredient lists here that contain chicken feet.

You can be sure that the following recipes have been tried and tested hundreds, if not thousands, of times. They are sure to please your family as much as they have pleased our guests over the years. No substitutions needed.

Oh yeah, to wash it all down? Try some of Wisconsin's most famous beverage—beer. And when you are in the Milwaukee vicinity, be sure to visit one of the breweries for a tour and tasting.

Yankee Pot Roast

Serves 6

---

4 to 5 pounds boneless chuck roast,
    1½ inches thick

½ cup oil

2 cups water

½ teaspoon salt

½ teaspoon black pepper, freshly ground

3 bay leaves

1 pound red potatoes

1 large Spanish onion

1 pound carrots

3 stalks celery

Coating

½ cup flour

1 teaspoon dried parsley, crushed

1 teaspoon dried thyme, crushed

Gravy

6 tablespoons margarine

⅓ cup flour

For coating, mix the flour, parsley, and thyme in a shallow pan. Coat the roast with the flour mixture. Heat the oil in a frying pan big enough to hold the roast. Add the flour-coated roast, browning it on both sides. Remove roast from frying pan to roaster and add 2 cups water. Sprinkle roast with salt, pepper, and the bay leaves. Cover and cook for 1 hour in 325° F. oven. Meanwhile, scrub the potatoes and cut in half; peel carrots and onions and cut in 1½" pieces; cut celery in 1½" pieces as well. Remove roaster from oven after 1 hour of cooking and add the carrots, potatoes, onion, and celery, placing them on top of and around the meat in an even layer. Replace cover and return to oven. For a 4-pound roast, cook 1½ hours more. If the roast is closer to 5 pounds, cook for 2 hours more. Once done, the roast can sit in a turned-off oven for up to 30 minutes.

A half hour before you are ready to serve, remove the meat from the roaster and slice in ¼" slices. Arrange on large platter, surrounded by vegetables. Cover and keep warm in oven while you make the gravy.

Strain the juice left in the roaster to remove bay leaves and other solids. In saucepan over medium heat, melt the margarine, add the flour, and stir with a whisk until a roux is formed (a mixture that is well combined and smooth). Continue to cook over medium heat and add all of the strained juice plus enough water to make 3 cups. Add the liquid slowly while stirring for an absolutely lump-free gravy. Keep warm over low heat until served.

Pierogi

Makes 2 dozen

Dough

1 large egg

¼ cup salad oil

¾ cup lukewarm water

3 cups flour

1 teaspoon salt

In bowl, whisk together egg, oil, and water. Add flour and salt; stir with spoon until a soft ball of dough is formed. Knead until smooth, adding additional flour only if necessary for ball to form. Cover dough and let rest 30 or 40 minutes while you prepare the filling.

Filling

*¾ cup potatoes, mashed smooth
(leftovers work well)*

½ cup grated cheddar cheese

¼ cup sour cream

¼ teaspoon white pepper

dash of nutmeg

½ teaspoon salt

Blend all ingredients together with a spoon.

Egg Wash

1 egg, beaten

1 tablespoon water

Pierogi, *continued*

To assemble pierogi

Beat egg and water together to form an egg wash. Divide dough in half. Roll out each half about ⅛" thick. Using a round cookie cutter or a glass that is 3"–4" in diameter, cut out as many circles as you can. Remove extra dough and set aside. Place one heaping tablespoon of filling in the center of each circle. Brush the edges of each circle with the egg wash. Fold the circle in half, sealing the edges together with your fingers. Continue with the other half of dough. If you still have filling left, combine the dough scraps and knead into one ball. Roll out and use up the rest of the filling. Otherwise, these scraps can be cut up into pieces as noodles for soup or as a side dish.

To cook the pierogi

Bring a pot of water to a boil. Add the *pierogi* and cook until the dough is done, about 5 minutes. If the *pierogi* were frozen when you put them in the water, they will float to the top when they are done. Turn *pierogi* over to make sure both sides get cooked. Drain. You can serve them as is or sauté them in a little butter and parsley. This is the absolute best! Just brown them a little in the butter and serve with sour cream on the side.

You can easily quadruple this recipe to make 8 dozen *pierogi* at a time. They freeze quite well. Just lay the uncooked *pierogi* individually on a cookie sheet and set in the freezer until the *pierogi* are very firm or frozen. Store in a container, placing waxed paper between layers. When you want to cook some, take out the amount you want and cook per the directions.

Irish Soda Bread

Makes 1 loaf or 8 individual rolls

2 cups flour

2 cups whole-wheat flour

2 teaspoons baking soda

1½ teaspoons cream of tartar

4 tablespoons margarine

1½ cups buttermilk

In a bowl, sift the flours with the baking soda and cream of tartar. Cut in the margarine to form a crumbly mixture. Add buttermilk and beat to form a soft dough. Turn out onto a floured counter and knead for just 1 minute, until a smooth ball of dough is formed. Shape this into a nice round, then cut a cross into the top. You have to cut quite deeply for it to show up once it is baked. Bake in a preheated 400° F. oven for 45 minutes. The bread will be lightly browned and firm when tapped. Serve warm with homemade preserves.

If you prefer to make individual rolls, cut the dough into 8 even portions. Repeat the shaping technique. Bake in a preheated 400° F. oven for about 20 minutes.

Blueberry Blintzes

Serves 8

8 crepe shells (recipe, Chapter 1)

2 cups blueberry pie filling (recipe follows)

3 tablespoons butter

3 tablespoons margarine

1 cup crème fraîche

Lay out the crepe shells on your counter and divide the blueberry pie filling evenly among them, placing the filling in the center of each. In a large sauté pan, melt the butter and margarine together and turn to low. To make the blintz, roll up each shell by folding in half over the filling; then take each side and fold in, turning the finished blintz over to place the seam on the bottom. Place each blintz seam side down in the sauté pan and brown lightly. Turn over and repeat, to brown each side lightly. Remove and drain on paper toweling. Serve warm with a heaping tablespoon of *crème fraîche*.

Blueberry Pie Filling

Makes about 4 cups

4 cups fresh blueberries

3 tablespoons quick-cooking tapioca

½ cup sugar

juice of 1 lemon

Wash the blueberries and drain. Blend the tapioca with the sugar and pour over the blueberries. Add the strained lemon juice. Gently mix all ingredients together and let sit for 15 minutes. Cook in the top half of a double boiler for 20 minutes, stirring often, but gently, so as to not crush the blueberries. Cool and refrigerate. Will keep for a week.

Blueberry Blintzes, continued

Crème Fraîche
Makes 1 cup

Only the name sounds difficult. This is often the best complement to a sweet or very rich dessert, having a tart flavor and creamy texture.

½ cup whipping cream

½ cup sour cream

Whisk the creams together in a small ceramic or glass bowl. (Do not use aluminum or copper.) Cover tightly with plastic wrap and let stand for about 12 hours in a warm place. If you have a gas oven, the top of the stove above a pilot light is a good spot. Constant warmth, not direct heat is what you want. Now, stir the mixture and refrigerate it for 24 hours, the time necessary to allow the flavors and enzymes to develop .

Chapter Six

Great Lakes Fish Fry

U p north in Wisconsin they have the fish boil. Down here in our section of the state, we have the Friday-night fish fry. Almost every restaurant in the area offers its own version of this great event.

But the best fish fry is also the simplest. And the finest eating fish ever to come out of water, in my opinion, is the common bluegill. Fillet a batch and pan fry 'em for a great-tasting breakfast, lunch, or (Friday night) dinner.

Fishing is not only a great way to procure a meal you'll be proud of, but it also excels as a solitary activity. It gives you time to think and ponder life's little mysteries and as a social activity, it creates memories that last much longer than a delicious meal.

My younger brother, John, was a master fisherman. To me, that means that he could catch fish no matter what, in any weather. And nothing could stop him from fishing, his favorite activity. A lot of my memories of him are surrounded by fishing.

If you've gone fishing even once, you have at least one good memory of it and everyone seems to have a favorite fish story. My dad's involves my brothers, John and Bob. If Dad and John

Pan Fried Bluegills,
Tartar Sauce

Crunchy Coleslaw

Potato Pancakes

Homemade Ice Cream with
Mocha Fudge Sauce

wanted to catch a goodly amount of fish, they went by themselves; if they wanted to have a good laugh, they invited brother Bob along.

One day the three were out together, and John was catching all the fish (I told you he was a master fisherman!), while Bob wasn't catching a thing. Sitting out there in the boat in the middle of the lake, Bob's lack of luck was gettin' to him. So what did he do but dive in—to see where all those fish were! Well, he didn't find any on that side of the surface either.

But if you're persistent, if the weather is right, and if you have the right bait, you will find your share of bluegills in any one of the many lakes we are blessed with in Wisconsin.

And even though the details and intricacies of catching fish are better left to master fishermen, I do know about cooking 'em. Start with freshly caught and cleaned fish, then just follow these recipes.

It is not unusual for people to eat so much fish that they have no room left for dessert. In cases like that, homemade ice cream is in order. Gives you a little exercise too, turning that crank. Just be sure to let everyone have a turn.

Pan-Fried Bluegills (or other panfish)

Serves 2 hungry fishermen

1 ½ pounds fish fillets

½ cup milk

1 egg

½–¾ cup cooking oil, preferably
    polyunsaturated

Coating mix

¾ cup flour

¼ cup yellow cornmeal

1 teaspoon dried parsley, crushed

½ teaspoon dried thyme, crushed

¼ teaspoon white pepper

1 teaspoon paprika

½ teaspoon onion powder

¼ teaspoon salt, optional

In heavy frying pan, heat ½" oil to 350°–375° F. Mix milk and egg together and beat well. For coating mix, combine dry ingredients in bowl and mix together. Dredge fillets first in the milk and egg mixture, then in coating mix, patting the fillets firmly into the latter to get a good coat. Place a single layer of fillets in a hot frying pan and cook 1 to 2 minutes on each side, watching carefully. Remove fillets with slotted spoon and drain on paper towel. Keep warm in oven, uncovered, while you cook the rest of the fillets. Serve with tartar sauce if desired.

Tartar Sauce

Makes about 1 cup

¾ cup mayonnaise or salad dressing

¼ cup pickle relish

1 tablespoon lemon juice

1 tablespoon yellow mustard

Mix all ingredients together. Keep refrigerated.

Crunchy Coleslaw

Serves 6–8

1 head green cabbage (1½ – 2 pounds)

1 carrot

1 green pepper

1 medium Spanish onion

½ cup sesame seeds

½ cup currants

½ cup pine nuts

Grate cabbage, carrot, green pepper, and onion on fine side of grater and combine in bowl. Toss with sesame seeds, currants, and pine nuts. Pour dressing over entire mixture and toss. Serve well chilled.

Dressing

½ cup mayonnaise

½ cup sour cream

¼ cup maple syrup

juice of 1 lemon, strained

¼ teaspoon salt (optional)

⅛ teaspoon white pepper

Whip together mayonnaise and sour cream. Add maple syrup, lemon juice, salt, and pepper. Whip all ingredients together once again. Dressing will keep for 3 or 4 days, refrigerated.

Potato Pancakes

Serves 10

2 cups potatoes, peeled and grated fine

½ cup onion, peeled and grated fine

2 eggs, beaten

2 tablespoons flour

½ teaspoon salt

¼ teaspoon baking powder

1 teaspoon dried parsley, crushed

oil for cooking

The secret of these pancakes is to hand-grate the potatoes really fine. This will produce a lot of liquid. Place the grated potatoes and the juice, all of it, in a bowl. Add the grated onion and beaten eggs and mix together. Combine flour, salt, baking powder, and parsley and sprinkle over the mixture. Combine all ingredients. Heat about ¼" of cooking oil in a heavy pan over moderately hot fire. Spoon three or four pancakes into the oil, flattening them out slightly to form an oval. Cook on both sides until browned. Remove from oil with slotted spoon or spatula and drain on paper toweling. Keep warm in oven, uncovered, while you make up the rest. Serve with applesauce, maple syrup, or sour cream.

Homemade Ice Cream

What a treat! These directions are for ice cream made with an old-fashioned wooden freezer—the kind you hand-crank. The basic recipe can be used for other types of ice-cream makers as well—just follow the manufacturer's instructions.

The basic ingredients in ice cream are cream, sugar, and flavoring. In order to produce a smooth ice cream, the ice crystals that form in it must be kept very small. This is done by adding ingredients that prevent large crystals from forming—such as eggs, fruit, and nuts.

In ice creams that are made by churning, the amount of air whipped in depends on the speed at which the churn is turned and the temperature at which the mixture is frozen. As the ice melts, it absorbs heat from the ice cream and lowers the temperature of the mixture. The rate of melting is controlled by the proportion of salt to ice. A mix of 1 part rock salt to 10 parts ice produces the best-textured ice cream.

In preparation for ice-cream making, scald the freezer can and dasher.

Next, prepare the ice-cream mixture and pour into the freezer can. The can should be no more than three-fourths full to allow for expansion. Center the can in the freezer container, adjust the dasher, and cover.

Pack the correct proportion of crushed ice and rock salt around the can.

Turn the dasher slowly until the ice melts enough for you to see some liquid. Add more ice and salt as you go, keeping the lid just covered.

Turn the handle fast and steady until it becomes tougher to turn. After removing enough ice to allow you to take the lid off, remove the dasher. Replace the lid and cover the opening in the lid with plastic wrap and fit several layers of foil tightly over the entire lid.

Pack more ice and salt around the can to fill the freezer completely. Cover the freezer with a heavy blanket or two. Lots of newspapers work well, too. Let ice cream ripen for 4 hours. This is the hardest part—waiting to eat it!

You will need about 20 pounds of ice and 2 pounds of rock salt to make a gallon of ice cream.

Old Fashioned Vanilla Ice Cream

1½ cups sugar

2 tablespoons flour

½ teaspoon salt

4 cups half and half

4 eggs, beaten

4 cups whipping cream

2 tablespoons vanilla extract

In stockpot, combine sugar, flour, and salt. Slowly stir in the half and half, whisking with a wire whip to combine. Add the beaten eggs and mix together. Cook over medium heat, stirring constantly for about 10 minutes or until mixture has thickened slightly. Remove from heat and cool. Stir in the whipping cream and vanilla. Chill completely. When you are ready to make ice cream, pour into the 1-gallon can of your ice cream freezer and follow basic procedures. Serve with hot Mocha Fudge Sauce.

Mocha Fudge Sauce
Makes 2 cups

4 ounces unsweetened chocolate squares

2 tablespoons butter

⅔ cup coffee, very hot but not boiling

2 cups sugar

2 tablespoons corn syrup

In the top half of a double boiler, melt the chocolate and butter. Stir in the hot coffee, then add sugar and corn syrup. Cook for about 5 minutes, stirring occasionally, at a near boil (steam evaporating, but no broken bubbles on the surface). Serve hot. Once the sauce has cooled, you may reheat it in the microwave or in a saucepan on the stove. Keeps well in covered jar in the refrigerator.

Chapter Seven

Bluegrass Picnic

The Greene House Country Inn is home to the Guitar Gallery, where you can shop for collectable guitars, banjos, and miscellaneous accouterments. Musicians and collectors walk in almost every day.

And, of course, they stop to play these instruments every so often. You never know just whom you will get to meet or hear: Bobbi McFerrin to Randy Bachman, Piper Road Spring Band to Charlie Edmunds, Sesame Street to hot commercial hits, bluegrass to the blues.

You may think it a bit unusual at first, this collection of unique instruments for sale or trade. But then you will be informed: Les Paul's hometown is just up the road. And Liberace's. Alpine Valley is an outdoor music theater that has seen the likes of the Rolling Stones, Jimmy Buffet, and everyone in between.

There's a blues club down the road and a little bit farther, you will find the Cafe Carpe, setting up the best in folk music. At Milwaukee's Shank Hall, you can catch Arlo Guthrie or the latest in fusion jazz. And at the University of Wisconsin, Whitewater, everything sounds great in the Irving Young Auditorium.

Whole Wheat Bread

Homemade Chicken Salad

Vegetarian Sandwich Filling

Perfect Potato Salad

Roman Apple Cake

In the good old summertime, there is a Bluegrass Festival on the green grass of the nearby town of East Troy. You can set yourself down there and take a load off. The atmosphere is so homespun you may think you're in Mayberry.

But don't just be part of the crowd. Borrow a guitar, a banjo, or a dobro from Mayner's collection and become a part of the celebration. Just be sure to pack a picnic lunch, because you're bound for an all-day affair.

To grant you the energy to play all day, we've included the best of home-made breads, two sandwich fixin's, potato salad on the side, and a packable apple cake for dessert. There won't be any leftovers on this picnic.

Whole Wheat Bread

Makes 2 loaves

---

2 packages yeast

1 tablespoon sugar

2 cups warm water, 110° F.

1 egg, beaten

¼ cup salad oil

1 cup milk warmed to 100–110° F.

1 teaspoon salt

¼ cup honey

4 cups whole-wheat flour

4–5 cups all-purpose flour

In bread bowl, pour in water and 1 tablespoon sugar. Add yeast and whip mixture to dissolve yeast. Let yeast work. When a puffy, gray-brown cloud of foam has formed, you are ready to proceed. Add the egg, oil, milk, salt, and honey. Next, add whole-wheat flour and mix. Add 4 cups of the bread flour gradually, mixing together to form a spongy dough. Turn dough out on floured counter and knead, using up the remaining cup of bread flour. Let rise once in bowl. Form 2 loaves and let rise again. Bake bread in 400° F. oven for 15 minutes; then turn down heat to 350° F. and continue baking for 25 minutes longer.

Homemade Chicken Salad

Makes enough filling for 6 sandwiches

2 cups cooked chicken, diced*

½ cup diced celery

¼ cup diced onion

½ cup canned crushed pineapple, drained

½ cup slivered almonds

½ cup mayonnaise

½ cup sour cream

¼ cup maple syrup

½ teaspoon salt

⅛ teaspoon white pepper

½ teaspoon Hungarian paprika

juice of ½ lemon

Combine chicken, celery, onion, pineapple, and almonds in mixing bowl. In separate bowl, whip together mayonnaise, sour cream, and maple syrup. Add salt, pepper, and paprika. Add strained lemon juice. Mix these ingredients well and pour over the chicken mixture. Mix together and chill.

*The chicken should be diced quite small, but do not use a food processor, as this ends up mashing it, creating quite a different texture. You may substitute cooked turkey for the chicken.

Vegetarian Sandwich Filling

Makes enough filling for 6 sandwiches

1 pound cream cheese

½ pound cheddar cheese, grated

¼ cup minced green pepper

¼ cup minced onion

¼ cup shredded carrot

½ cup sliced black olives

4 ounces mushrooms, sliced

2 eggs, hard cooked and diced (optional)

½ cup sunflower seeds

¼ cup currants

In mixer bowl, combine cheese and beat on low speed. Add pepper, onion, and carrot and mix together. Remove from mixer and stir in olives, mushrooms, eggs, sunflower seeds, and currants. Chill completely. (When making sandwiches, top this mixture with a sprinkling of alfalfa sprouts.)

To Make Picnic Sandwiches

Slice 2 pieces of whole-wheat bread and butter both slices lightly. (The butter keeps the bread from getting soggy.) On 1 slice, place a piece of lettuce, top with tomato slices or cheese if desired, then ½ cup sandwich filling. Top with second slice of bread. Cut sandwich in half and wrap in plastic wrap or foil. Refrigerate.

Perfect Potato Salad

Serves 6

3 cups boiled potatoes, peeled while warm
and sliced ¼" thick

2 hard-cooked eggs, sliced

¼ cup finely chopped onion

½ cup finely chopped celery

½ cup mayonnaise

1 tablespoon lemon juice

2 tablespoons sugar

dash of white pepper

dash of salt

Combine first four ingredients. To make dressing, combine remaining ingredients in separate bowl and mix well. Pour dressing over potatoes and stir. Refrigerate, covered, for at least 2 hours. The secret to perfect potato salad is using freshly cooked potatoes that are slightly warm when you mix the salad together. This causes all the flavors to meld together. Keep refrigerated.

Roman Apple Cake

Makes a 9" x 13" cake

½ cup butter

½ cup margarine

1 cup sugar

½ cup brown sugar

2 large eggs

1 cup buttermilk (or substitute sour milk or yogurt)

2½ cups flour

½ teaspoon salt

1 teaspoon baking powder

1 teaspoon baking soda

1 tablespoon cinnamon

1 pound apples

In mixer, cream together butter, margarine, and sugars; add eggs and mix. In separate bowl, combine dry ingredients and add to creamed mixture alternately with buttermilk. The batter will be a bit thick. Wash apples, core, and grate medium fine, with the skin on. Add the apples to the batter and mix thoroughly. Pour into a greased and floured 9" x 13" pan. Top with streusel. Bake in a preheated 300° F. oven for 1 hour. Once cake is cooled, top with sifted powdered sugar if desired. This cakes gets better with a day's aging. Serve as is or with a dollop of whipped cream.

Streusel Topping

Makes 2 cups streusel

¾ cup flour

½ cup sugar

¼ cup butter

½ cup margarine

½ cup quick-cooking oatmeal

In mixing bowl, combine flour and sugar. Cut in butter and margarine with pastry cutter or fork to make a crumbly mixture. Add oatmeal and cut in. Will keep if stored in airtight bags in freezer.

Chapter Eight

Puttin' on the Grill

One fine place to be in the summertime is on the deck, lounging while someone you love cooks up dinner on the grill.

The secret to successful lounging is to make sure that the entire dinner comes from the grill. Fewer dishes, less fuss. Of course, you do have to hand out more accolades. But that's easy: Everything cooked this way ends up tasting great. So praise away.

The following menu is not only easy to cook on the grill, it is easy to prepare. So get plannin'. Then lounge around while your grilling guru goes to work.

Hot Spinach and
Bacon Salad

Grilled Smoked Turkey Breast
with Basting Sauces

Vegetable Kabobs

Caramelized Fruit over
Baked Custard

Hot Spinach and Bacon Salad

Serves 6

6 cups washed and cleaned spinach leaves

6 ounces bacon (10 – 12 slices)

1 small onion, diced

½ cup croutons

1 teaspoon Dijon mustard

3 tablespoons grated Parmesan cheese

2 tablespoons olive oil

⅓ cup red wine vinegar

3 tablespoons sugar

6 hard-cooked eggs, sliced

Place spinach in serving bowl and set aside. Chop bacon in small pieces and place in sauté pan with onions. Set on grill rack and fry until bacon is crisp. Add croutons and stir until croutons are coated with bacon and onions. In separate bowl, whisk together mustard, Parmesan cheese, olive oil, vinegar, and sugar and add to sauté pan. Cook until just hot. Pour over spinach, add the sliced eggs, toss, and serve immediately.

Grilled Smoked Turkey Breast

Serves 12

1 turkey breast, 8 to 10 pounds

1 charcoal grill with lid

1 grilling guru

1 recipe basting sauce

Grilling is best done by those you want to keep out of the kitchen. In my case, that's Mayner. And he has lots of experience at the grill. Here are his 10 tips for a really tasty turkey breast, juicy and full of flavor.

1) You will need at least 5 pounds of charcoal. (A good rule of thumb is half the weight of the turkey in coals; a 10-pound turkey breast will require 5 pounds of charcoal.) You will need to add coals as you cook.

2) Use a mixture of hickory coals and regular briquettes for the best flavor.

3) Throw in a little maple or apple wood if you have it.

4) Stack your coals in a pyramid shape on one side of the grill. Let them get good and hot.

5) The rack should be an inch or two above the coals.

6) Put turkey directly above the coals and brown on all sides, turning frequently. You have to watch it closely at this stage. Browning first like this helps to seal in the juice and flavor for the rest of the cooking time.

7) Finish cooking through the use of indirect heat: Move the turkey to the center of the grill and turn it every 30 minutes until done. A 10-pound turkey breast will take about 2 ½ hours. A tight-fitting lid is essential to the smoking process and should be kept on until the turkey is done.

8) Keep the bottom vent open all the way. If your grill has lid vents, keep them half open. This will give you enough smoke to flavor the bird.

9) You need to keep the grill hot. Add more coals as you cook to keep the temperature constant. The colder the outside temperature, the more difficult it can be to keep a uniform temperature.

10) Use a meat thermometer to test the turkey by sticking it into the thickest part of the breast. When the internal temperature reaches 165° F., the meat is done. Remove from grill and keep warm, letting it rest at least 15 minutes before slicing.

Grilled Smoked Turkey Breast, continued

Apple Cider Glaze

1 cup apple cider

½ cup maple syrup

1 teaspoon fresh lemon juice

Mix together and brush on turkey for the last hour of cooking.

Cranberry Basting Sauce

1 cup whole-berry cranberry sauce

½ cup orange marmalade

½ cup honey

Mix ingredients together in saucepan and heat to a simmer. Stir to mix. Remove from heat and brush on turkey for the last hour of cooking time.

Vegetable Kabobs
Serves 6

12 skewers, wood or metal, at least
     10" long

24 small red potatoes

3 medium zucchini

1 pound fresh mushrooms

2 medium Spanish onions

2 green peppers

1 medium eggplant

6 ears fresh sweet corn

Wash and clean potatoes. Boil or microwave for 10 minutes to cook partially. Cut each zucchini into four pieces. Clean and wash mushrooms. Peel onions and cut into 1" cubes. Wash peppers, halve, remove seeds, and cut into 1" cubes. Peel eggplant, halve, and cut into 1" cubes. Shuck and clean sweet corn and cut each ear into four pieces. Assemble vegetables on skewers: potato, zucchini, mushroom, onion, pepper, eggplant, corn, etc., until all vegetables are skewered. Brush each kabob with marinating sauce and keep refrigerated until ready to grill. To grill, place about 2" from the charcoal and turn frequently, basting with remaining sauce. Cook on grill for approximately 30 minutes, or until corn is tender.

Marinating Sauce

½ cup corn oil

¼ cup honey

3 cloves garlic, crushed

1 tablespoon chopped fresh thyme,
     or 1 teaspoon dried

1 tablespoon chopped fresh parsley,
     or 1 teaspoon dried

¼ teaspoon freshly ground black pepper

Combine all ingredients and blend well. Refrigerate until needed. This will keep for several weeks.

Caramelized Fruit Over Baked Custard

Serves 6

½ cup butter

½ cup brown sugar

2 bananas

2 baking apples

2 pears

½ cup currants

Melt butter in ovenproof pan on grill rack. Add brown sugar and stir until melted. Slice bananas and add to pan. Peel and slice apples and pears and add to pan. Cook the fruit, stirring occasionally, in the butter and sugar mixture. The pan should be about 2" to 4" above the hot coals. When the apples are tender (test with a fork), add the currants and toss. Serve warm over baked custard. Garnish with whipped cream if desired.

Baked Custard

6 whole eggs

½ cup brown sugar

¼ teaspoon salt (optional)

¼ teaspoon nutmeg

2 cups milk

2 tablespoons rum

In mixing bowl, beat eggs until frothy. Add brown sugar, salt, and nutmeg and mix to incorporate. Add milk and rum and beat. Pour into lightly greased and floured pie pan (9" to 10") and bake in preheated 350° F. oven for 20 to 30 minutes or until a knife inserted in center comes out clean. Slice into 6 wedges and serve with caramelized fruit.

Chapter Nine

Farmers' Market Buffet

There is a time of year in Wisconsin when even the friendliest people start locking their back doors, their car doors, even their garage doors. It happens about two weeks into the zucchini harvest.

Because people have found out that if they forget to lock those doors, they will be visited upon by a big bag of . . . zucchini! Just left there, sometimes without so much as a note.

Wisconsin is a land of gardeners. And even if you plant only one package of the prolific zucchini, you are bound to have too many. And since Wisconsin gardeners are thrifty, it pains them to throw anything away. So they pick all those green vegetables, bag them, and then strive to give them away. Deep into harvest time, they have been known to give them to complete strangers!

Just down the road from our place, the general store has a bag full of zucchini sitting right there, with a big old "FREE" sign on it.

So, you can understand why people in Wisconsin sometimes lock their doors. It's not that they're unfriendly; they're just thinking ahead.

For folks not lucky enough to have their own garden plots, there are plenty of farmers' markets to wander through. In these

Cabbage Patch Soup

Farmers' Market Salad

Freezer-Batter Zucchini Bread

Apple Tart

67

wondrous places of slick-looking, freshly picked vegetables and fruits, you can
find green beans in every shape and
color, bushels of snap peas, bags of
tomatoes in reds and yellows, and winter
squash so unusual they look as if they
came from outer space instead of garden

space. You can buy most anything
here—even zucchini, if they haven't
started to give it away yet.

Cabbage Patch Soup

Makes 10 cups

1 cup dried black-eyed peas

10 cups water

2 cups grated cabbage

1 cup chopped carrots

1 cup chopped potatoes

2 cups crushed tomatoes

½ cup chopped onions

2 bay leaves

1 teaspoon dried thyme, crushed

1 teaspoon dried marjoram, crushed

1 tablespoon dried parsley, crushed

1 teaspoon granulated garlic, or
    ½ teaspoon garlic powder

½ teaspoon freshly ground black pepper

2 tablespoons molasses

salt (optional)

In stockpot, cover the black-eyed peas with the water and soak overnight in the refrigerator. The next day, bring soaked peas to a boil, then lower heat to a simmer and add all remaining ingredients except molasses. Remove a little liquid from the stockpot, mix with the molasses, and add the mixture back to stockpot. (If you don't mix the molasses this way, it will just sit at the bottom of the pot.) Simmer, uncovered, for 2 hours. Adjust seasoning with salt, if desired.

Farmers' Market Salad
Serves 4

This makes a wonderfully lively salad, glowing with many colors of the garden. The nasturtium flower is perfectly edible, with a slightly peppery taste. If you prefer, use the flowers to garnish the finished salad.

2 cups cooked pasta, any kind

1 small red pepper

1 small green pepper

1 zucchini

¼ pound green beans, cut in 2″ pieces

½ cup broccoli florettes

¼ pound pea pods

1 large yellow tomato

1 large red tomato

½ cup nasturtium blossoms (optional)

Dressing

juice of 1 lemon

¼ cup red wine vinegar

⅔ cup light olive oil

½ teaspoon salt (optional)

½ teaspoon freshly ground black pepper

¼ cup minced chives

Place the cooked pasta in large mixing bowl. Clean vegetables, pat dry with paper toweling, and cut into bite-sized pieces. Add to pasta and toss to combine.

In separate bowl make the dressing. Whisk together the strained lemon juice and the vinegar. Drizzle olive oil slowly into mixture, whisking to incorporate. Add remaining ingredients and whisk. Pour dressing over pasta and toss to combine. Serve well chilled. This salad tastes best when left to age for about 2 hours.

Freezer-Batter Zucchini Bread

Makes 3 mini-loaves or 12 muffins

4 eggs

2 cups sugar

1 cup salad oil

2 cups zucchini, freshly grated, skin on

1 teaspoon vanilla

1 teaspoon salt

1 ½ teaspoons cinnamon

1 teaspoon baking soda

1 ¼ teaspoons double-acting
    baking powder*

2¾ cups flour

Cream together eggs, sugar, and oil. Add zucchini and vanilla and blend. Sift together dry ingredients and mix as you add. Once all dry ingredients are incorporated, turn off mixer and remove bowl of batter.

Variation 1: Add ½ cup chopped nuts and ½ cup raisins

Variation 2: For chocolate zucchini batter (it's good!), add ½ cup cocoa and 2 tablespoons softened butter

Freeze batter by storing in a resealable container. If you make a large batch, you can even use a recycled plastic ice-cream bucket with lid. These will stack in your freezer neatly. Be sure to mark with contents.

*This recipe was formulated specifically for freezing. Almost all baking powder on the market now is double-acting—but do check to be sure. The "double-acting" refers to its ability to act twice—once when you add it to your other ingredients, once when it becomes heated in the baking process. If you make this batter for immediate baking, decrease the amount of baking powder by ¼ teaspoon.

Apple Tart

Serves 8

1 recipe sweet tart pastry dough

2 pounds tart baking apples

1 cup drained canned elderberries
    (or fresh raspberries)

¾ cup red jam or jelly –(raspberry
    works well)

whipped cream for topping, if desired

To assemble tart, peel, core, and slice apples. Arrange slices on top of dough in pan. Sprinkle the elderberries on top of apples. Melt the jam or jelly and pour evenly on top of apples. Bake in 350° F. oven for about 30 minutes. The apples should be tender and the crust lightly browned. Serve with whipped cream.

Sweet Tart Pastry Dough

¾ cup flour

3 tablespoons sugar

pinch of salt

3 tablespoons butter

2 large egg yolks, slightly beaten

⅛ teaspoon vanilla

In bowl, combine flour, sugar, and salt. Cut butter in to form crumbly mixture. Add egg yolks and vanilla. Stir together until you have a firm dough. Chill for at least 30 minutes. Roll out and line a 9" tart pan.

Chapter Ten

Jammin' Time

At our Country Inn, jammin' time is more than just making jam. It also refers to those impromptu music sessions that pop up now and again. The best of both worlds is when I'm in the big old country kitchen making up batches of sweet-smelling jam and there's music going on in the front hallway.

And when the music is over and the players are ready to leave, they say something like "We have to do this again!" What they really mean is, "When can we come back to taste that great-smelling jam?"

Either way, there is nothing quite so relaxing as listening to some good music while you putter around putting up preserves.

Most people don't know that you can make jam any time of the year. It doesn't have to be just during strawberry season (although that is still everyone's favorite).

I do tend to start out the jamming season with the strawberries—June or July for our part of the country. But then I move into raspberries, adding other fruits in order to stretch the wonderful taste even further. After that, I take a break from jam to put up other preserves and pickles.

Strawberry Sauce

Sugarless Strawberry Jam

Cranberry Cherry Sauce

Apple Jam

Orange Marmalade

It's back to jam with the apple harvest in October. This is such a nice time of year: The kitchen is a little cooler, and a batch of apple jam cooking just smells like fall. Cook some in the early morning and the chill is gone from the kitchen for the rest of the day.

Once the Thanksgiving holidays have come and gone, I get out the jars and lids once again, this time to take advantage of the fresh fruit available from other areas. Cranberries are usually plentiful this time of year. And orange marmalade is one of my favorites. It's great on breads and muffins, but can also be used as part of a basting sauce for meats.

So, get that music going. Grab your pots and jars and start a jammin' session of your own.

Strawberry Sauce
Makes about 4 pints

I like to make a goodly amount of this every year because it is so versatile. You can use it for a topping on ice cream or cereal. Combine it with soy sauce and BBQ sauce for a really nice teriyaki glaze. Add it to the blender for strawberry shakes or mix it into a basic muffin batter for a fruited treat in the morning.

Keep in mind that the yield of this recipe will vary, depending on the water content of the fruit.

8 cups strawberries, washed, hulled, and sliced

2 cups sugar

1 tablespoon lemon juice

Place all ingredients in a heavy kettle. Bring to a slow simmer and cook, stirring, for 10 minutes. Remove from heat and ladle the sauce into sterilized pint or half-pint jars. Leaving ½" headroom, screw on sterilized lids and tops. Process in a boiling-water bath for 10 minutes for pint jars, 8 minutes for half-pints. Remove jars, tighten lids, and let cool on wire rack.

Sugarless Strawberry Jam

Just because you can't have sugar, you shouldn't have to deprive yourself of strawberry jam. But making sugarless jam is tricky. You can do it using unflavored gelatin, but the result will be a jam that can be stored only in the refrigerator, since it would break down in a hot water bath. The easiest thing is to make small batches throughout the growing season and store them in the refrigerator.

You should crush the strawberries instead of slicing them. Be sure to use a liquid sweetener—the granular types tend to clump. (There are many artificial sweeteners now; your doctor should be able to tell which is best for you.)

Buy unflavored gelatin. The flavored kind has sweeteners already added which will throw off the recipe, and the artificial colors tend to look, well, artificial.

4 cups strawberries, cleaned, hulled, and crushed

8 teaspoons unflavored gelatin

3 tablespoons lemon juice

3–4 tablespoons liquid artificial sweetener

Place strawberries in heavy pan and heat to boiling. Meanwhile dissolve the gelatin in the lemon juice and sweetener. Remove berries from heat and add the remaining ingredients. Return to heat and bring to a boil once again. Remove from heat and ladle jam into four sterilized half-pint jars. Leave a scant ⅛-inch headroom. Screw on two-piece sterilized lids and let cool on wire rack. Refrigerate. Will keep 4 to 6 weeks if sealed. If one jar is short of jam, use that one first.

Cranberry Cherry Sauce
Makes 2 pints

This makes a wonderful alternative cranberry sauce for that Thanksgiving or Christmas turkey.

1 pound fresh or frozen whole cranberries

1 pound fresh cherries, pitted, or use 1 can (21 ounces) of cherry pie filling

3 cups sugar

Juice of 1 lemon

½ cup brandy

Coarsely grind cranberries or chop in a food processor. Put cranberries and juice in heavy stockpot. If using fresh cherries, grind coarsely and add to cranberries; if using the canned pie filling, add the entire contents of the can. Add sugar. Strain lemon juice to remove seeds and add along with the brandy. Bring to a boil while stirring, then reduce to a simmer and cook for 30 minutes, stirring frequently. Remove from heat, pour in jars, and seal with lids. Process in boiling-water bath for 10 minutes or store in refrigerator.

Apple Jam

Makes 4 pints

4 pounds cooking apples, about
    12 medium

8 cups sugar

2 whole lemons

4 whole cloves

1 stick cinnamon, broken up

Wash, peel, and core apples. Dice into small pieces. Combine apples, sugar, and the juice and zest of lemons in a large, heavy-bottomed kettle. Add a tea-leaves ball or spice bag filled with the whole cloves and stick cinnamon. Bring to a boil. Simmer for about 2 hours, stirring often, until set point is reached, 220° F. on a candy thermometer. Mixture will thicken quite a bit; do not add water. Once set point is reached, remove from heat and ladle into sterilized pint jars. Seal in boiling-water bath for 10 minutes or store in refrigerator.

Orange Marmalade

Makes 5 8-ounce jars

3 medium oranges

4 cups water

4 cups sugar

In a large, heavy kettle, 1 gallon in size or larger, cook the whole oranges and water at a simmer for about an hour and a half. The oranges are done when a fork may be inserted easily into them. Remove oranges from liquid and let cool. Cut oranges in half and remove pulp and seeds. Set aside the seeds for later. Using a sharp knife, cut the orange peel in very thin strips. Put seeds in tea-leaves ball or tie up in cheesecloth and add to liquid. Cook 10 minutes at a rapid boil. (The seeds aid in gelling.) Remove seeds. Add orange strips, bring mixture to a boil and cook for another 10 minutes at a rolling boil. Test for setting by checking temperature: your candy thermometer should read 220° F. When the setting temperature has been reached, remove kettle from heat, stir marmalade well, and let cool. When cooled, stir once again to distribute peel evenly and ladle into sterilized pint jars. Process in a boiling-water bath for 10 minutes or store in refrigerator. Be aware that you can lose the setting property of citrus fruits if you overcook, so test the temperature often.

Chapter Eleven

County Fair Favorites

The most important social event of the year in our rural, still mostly agricultural county is the county fair. Now over 135 years old, the fair is still looked forward to every Labor Day weekend.

As a kid, I remember working hard all year just to save up money to spend at the fair. Things haven't changed all that much. Back then, it was the midway that had me putting down my hard-earned money. Now, it might be a bag of books from the Historical Society's annual sale, over by the old log cabin and one-room schoolhouse. Or it might be a pair of hand-crocheted pillowcases from the senior-citizens booth.

And the food! All the stuff we never had at home as kids—corn dogs, taffy, elephant ears, cotton candy, and fudge. Now, you may want to pass those by for a real down-home dinner in one of the church tents or maybe a bowl of chili at the corner stand that has been there every year since I can remember.

If you come to the fair, save room for one of those deliciously sinful cream puffs. The money earned at this booth is almost the entire budget for the group of ladies that call themselves the Sweet Adelines. While standing in line (there are

Cinnamon Rolls

Church Tent Fried Chicken

Chuck Wagon Chili

Sweet Adelines Cream Puffs

always lines for something this good), you might hear them practicing their barbershop-style harmony.

On Labor Day Monday, get to the fairgrounds early to grab one of the best cinnamon rolls on earth, hot from the bakery truck right over there between the pavilion and the sheep barn. Bakers make the rolls as fast as they can and still run out. The smell alone is enough to make a person hungry.

Once you have a hot roll and a cup of coffee, head on over for the horse-pulling contest, in which teams of huge draft horses compete to see which can pull the most weight across the line. There are competitors from right in town as well as folks from farther away. You can help cheer on the local boys, but remember to stay quiet when the teams are pulling—you wouldn't want to risk a tongue lashing from the announcer.

After the horse pulling, there are harness racing and pig races—the winning pig gets an Oreo cookie. You can walk through the sheep and goat barn and look in on the mama pig and her brood in the swine barn. And try not to sound like a city slicker and call a steer a cow.

Then, check out the exhibition hall and find out who grew the tallest sunflower or the biggest pumpkin. Probably the same guy who won last year—what does he use for fertilizer?

When you are all tuckered out, sit yourself down in the grandstand for the best in country entertainment. And make a note to yourself to make reservations at our Country Inn for next year—because the rooms fill up fast for the world's best county fair!

Cinnamon Rolls

Makes 6 "Fair" size rolls

These are as good as they are big.

1 package yeast

½ cup water, 110° F.

1 tablespoon sugar

3 cups flour

2 teaspoons cinnamon

1 egg

⅓ cup milk, 110° F.

½ cup walnuts, finely ground

½ cup raisins

⅓ cup butter

½ cup brown sugar

In a small bowl, stir the yeast into the water and add sugar. Let dissolve. Let this mixture stand until the yeast starts foaming, about 5 minutes. In a large bread bowl, sift the flour and cinnamon together. Beat the egg and milk together and then add to the yeast mixture. Combine these liquids, then pour into the flour-cinnamon mixture and stir to form dough. Turn out onto a floured counter and knead to form a smooth ball. Flatten the dough out a little and sprinkle with the walnuts and raisins; continue kneading to incorporate them into the dough. Place dough in greased bowl, cover, and let rise until the dough has doubled in bulk. Punch down dough and turn out on floured counter. Roll out into a rectangular shape about 5" by 10". Melt the butter and brown sugar together and brush on the dough. Roll the dough up from a shorter end to form a log. Cut the dough into 8 pieces and lay each roll on a lightly greased and floured cookie sheet—2 across by 4 down. The rolls should be equally spaced with about ½" between them. Let rise until doubled in bulk. Bake in a preheated 325° F. oven for about 30 minutes. The rolls are done when lightly browned on the bottom and dry to the touch. Serve warm with a glass of fresh Wisconsin milk.

Church Tent Fried Chicken

Serves 4

1 frying chicken cut into 8 or 10 pieces

1 ½ cups flour

1 teaspoon black pepper

2 teaspoons salt

1 cup lard or frying oil

1 frying pan, extra deep to hold all the
    chicken, with lid

Wash chicken with clear, cold water and pat dry with a clean towel. Combine flour, pepper, and salt in bowl. Add lard or oil to frying pan and heat until a drop of flour will sizzle and brown. Roll each chicken piece in flour and place in hot oil in pan. Cook until crisp and brown, then turn the pieces and cook on other side. Add ½ cup water (carefully!), cover entire frying pan with lid, and simmer chicken until done, about 20 minutes. Remove lid and let chicken crisp up over a simmering heat. Remove chicken from pan and serve.

Chuck Wagon Chili

Serves 6 to 8

---

2 pounds ground beef

1 large onion, chopped fine

1 green pepper, chopped fine

3 cloves garlic, crushed

*1 large can crushed tomatoes
(28–30 ozs.), with juice*

*1 large can dark red kidney beans
(26–30 ozs.), with juice*

½ teaspoon salt

1 bay leaf

1 tablespoon chili powder

In cooking pot, brown the ground beef. Add the chopped onion, pepper, and garlic. Sauté, then drain fat if you wish. Add remaining ingredients and simmer, covered, for at least 1 hour. Serve with condiments on the side. Include chopped chili peppers, grated cheese, sour cream, and black olives. Plus cooked rice or pasta.

Sweet Adelines Cream Puffs

Makes 8 large cream puffs

1 cup water

½ cup butter

1 cup flour

4 eggs

½ pint whipping cream

¼ cup powdered sugar

In saucepan, bring the water to a boil. Add butter to water and heat until butter is melted. Remove pan from heat. Stir in flour until a globby ball forms. Do not overbeat. Add the eggs one at a time, stirring after each addition. Again, do not overbeat. After all eggs are added, you are ready to form the shells. Scoop out eight rounded spoonfuls, arranging them on an ungreased cookie sheet. Bake in a preheated 425° F. oven for about 20 minutes. The cream puffs are done when they are lightly browned, dry to the touch, and rather firm when you press down with your finger. Remove from oven and let cool. If you see the shells losing their puff, you did not cook them quite long enough.

Chill your mixing bowl in the freezer for about 15 minutes, then pour in whipping cream and beat until stiff peaks form. Slice each cream puff shell almost in half, keeping a "hinge" on it. Fill with a spoonful of whipped cream. Dust the tops of the cream puffs with powdered sugar. (You may use a can of ready-made whipping cream instead of whipping up your own. Instead of splitting the puffs, make a small hole with a knife in the top of the shell, insert the nozzle, and squirt in the whipped cream.)

Chapter Twelve

The Great Cookie Bakeoff

I don't know if my Mom started it or if she just got us started on it—this cookie-baking craze. All I know is that every year we would try to add one more variety to our holiday cookie list. Before reality set in, we were well over two dozen varieties. It was then we made the rule that if you made a new kind, you had to drop an old one. That was tough! They were all so good.

When I got my own place, my sisters and Mom were joined by extra friends I would invite over on a Sunday early in December to bake cookies. We baked all day, filling every container that had a lid. There were even enough cookies on the floor to keep the dogs happy for about a week.

We had eighty-year-old grandmas and five-year-old daughters bellying up to every table we could find. Thank goodness there was usually a football game on, since we didn't have room for the men. Of course, they came by every so often to check on us (eat cookies).

That was how the great Cookie Bakeoff started. It is a tradition that is sorely missed when for some reason we can't get a group together. It is the last really fun, just-for-ourselves party we do before the holidays hit hard.

Gingerbread Cookie Cutouts

Fruit Cake Gems

Rum Balls

*A Gingerbread House
    Of Your Own*

Cooked Eggnog

And the good part is you end up with a lot of cookies—to be served as midnight snacks, to fill cookie jars, to be packaged up prettily for hostess gifts, to be given to the mailman and the UPSer.

If you have little ones coming along for bakeoff day, it's a good idea to make up a gingerbread house for each one of them to decorate. Adding windows and doors and roof shingles will keep them busy, in case they get tired of frosting those Gingerbread Cookie Cutouts.

With all the cookies, you do need something to drink. Cookie-baking day usually means the first batch of eggnog. Made with a baked custard, it eliminates any worry about raw eggs. And it tastes just as good as the traditional eggnog, especially with a couple of cookies.

Gingerbread Cookie Cutouts

½ cup butter

½ cup margarine

2 cups brown sugar, packed

4 teaspoons baking soda

1 tablespoon salt

1 tablespoon cinnamon

1 teaspoon ginger

1 teaspoon cloves

1 teaspoon allspice

3 cups molasses

1⅓ cups water

12 cups flour

Cream butter, margarine, sugar, baking soda, salt, and spices together until fluffy. Mix in molasses and water. Gradually add flour. Dough will be quite stiff. Wrap dough tightly and refrigerate 2 hours or more. Roll out dough a little at a time to ¼" thick. Cut out cookies with shaped cutters and transfer to lightly greased baking sheet. Bake in 325° F. oven 10 to 15 minutes or until cookies are dry to the touch and a little brown on the bottom. Remove from baking sheet and let cool on a rack. When completely cool, ice and decorate.

Fruit-Cake Gems

Makes 8 dozen

1 cup butter

1 cup margarine

4 eggs

1 tablespoon rum extract

1 teaspoon vanilla extract

3 cups brown sugar

5 cups flour

2 teaspoons baking soda

2 teaspoons salt (optional)

1 tablespoon cinnamon

1 ½ cups candied fruit, minced

1 cup walnuts, coarsely chopped

1 cup almonds, coarsely chopped

1 cup dates, coarsely chopped

1 cup raisins or currants

In large bowl, cream the butter, margarine, eggs, brown sugar, and extracts. Sift the flour, baking soda, salt, and cinnamon together and stir into butter mixture by hand. Do not use an electric mixer, as it would make the cookies tough. Stir in remaining ingredients. Drop by teaspoonfuls onto lightly greased and floured cookie sheets. Set in freezer for 15 minutes. Bake in a preheated 350° F. oven until dry to the touch and lightly browned underneath. These are exceptionally good "keepers," as the fruit makes them very moist. Store in a tightly closed container with waxed paper between layers for up to 3 weeks. These cookies may be frozen.

Rum Balls

Makes 6 dozen

4 cups crushed vanilla wafers

2 cups finely ground pecans

2 cups powdered sugar

4 tablespoons cocoa

4 tablespoons maple syrup

⅔ cup dark rum

Extra 2 cups powdered sugar

In bowl, combine crushed vanilla wafers, pecans, powdered sugar, and cocoa. Stir in the maple syrup and dark rum to form a sticky mixture. Using a teaspoon, form 1-inch balls and roll them in the extra powdered sugar to coat. Store in a tightly sealed container for one week to develop flavor.

A Gingerbread House of Your Own

You will need:

1 batch Gingerbread Dough	assorted candy and candy canes
1 batch icing	icing bag and decorating tip
poster board	rolling pin
cardboard scraps	assorted cookie cutters
scissors	butcher paper

Gingerbread Dough

9 cups flour

1 tablespoon ground ginger

1 tablespoon allspice

1 teaspoon salt

2 large eggs

2 cups molasses

2 cups brown sugar, packed

2 cups margarine

2 teaspoons baking soda

Mix flour, spices, and salt in large bowl and set aside. In a heavy saucepan, combine molasses, brown sugar, margarine, and baking soda. Heat this mixture over medium heat and bring to a boil. Turn down heat and simmer for 5 minutes. Remove from heat and cool until just warm. Add eggs. Add this molasses mixture gradually to flour mixture, stirring until the whole is well combined. Leave in bowl and refrigerate at least 2 hours. Follow directions for cutting and baking the pieces.

A Gingerbread House of Your Own, continued

To cut and bake

Preheat oven to 350° F. This amount of gingerbread dough will make 2 houses, with enough dough left over for extra cookies. Each house requires 2 roof pieces, 2 side walls, and 2 end walls. Trace the house pattern on a piece of poster board or construction paper. Cut out pieces with scissors.

Take about a cup of the chilled dough and work it briefly with your hands to make it pliable. Shape into a rectangle and place on a well-floured counter. Roll the dough into a rectangular shape about ¼" thick. Try to achieve a uniform thickness. Lay the poster-board house pieces out on the dough. Using a sharp knife, cut around the pieces; remove poster-board. Pick up the dough pieces with a spatula and place them on an ungreased cookie sheet, keeping about ½" between pieces.

When you have cut out as many big pieces as you can, cut out some smaller pieces using cookie cutters. Some of the shapes that could be incorporated into your gingerbread scene are boys and girls, Santa figures, Christmas trees, stars, or cars. Make sure that you do not mix small and large pieces on one cookie sheet; the small pieces will bake faster than the larger pieces. When you have cut out as many pieces as you can, move the scrap dough aside and roll out another rectangle of dough; continue cutting out shapes. Finally, put the scrap pieces together and roll out.

Bake the gingerbread sections. The larger house pieces should take 10 to 15 minutes. Test for doneness by touching the gingerbread with your finger; if it is dry to the touch and "bounces back" instead of showing an indentation, it is done. Pull the cookie sheet out of the oven and check your pieces for accuracy before they cool completely. Do this by laying your pattern pieces on top of the baked gingerbread and trimming if necessary. This simple step will help assure that your house goes together without any kinks in the walls! Next, remove the baked gingerbread from the cookie sheets and transfer to a cake rack. Allow pieces to dry for 1 hour or more. (You could leave them in your turned-off oven overnight.)

A Gingerbread House of Your Own, continued

Icing

2 pounds confectioners sugar

6 large egg whites at room temperature

1 ½ teaspoons cream of tartar

Combine all ingredients in mixer bowl and beat on low speed until whites are incorporated. Then beat on high speed for 5 minutes. Wipe down the sides of the bowl occasionally with a spatula. Icing is done when peaks will stay stiff as you lift the spatula from the icing. Keep icing covered with a damp cloth until ready to use. (You may substitute 6 tablespoons meringue powder and ¾ cup water for the egg whites.)

To assemble house

Cut a 10" by 10" square out of heavy cardboard and cover with a piece of butcher paper. Tape the paper underneath one side of the cardboard—this will be the base for your house.

Take 1 baked end piece, pipe a row of icing along the bottom edge, and position it on your base. Next, take a side wall, pipe a row of icing along each of the side and bottom edges, and position it on your base, joining it to the end piece already in place—another pair of hands is helpful for this part or use a couple of coffee mugs to keep the pieces in place until the whole is put together. After you add the second side wall and the other end piece, you will have a house with no roof. Hold this in place until icing sets and it is firm enough to stand on its own.

To add the roof: Pipe a generous line of icing along the top edges of walls. Take one side of the roof and, making sure the overhang is the same on both sides of the house, gently push down on the roof piece to join it to the house. Now pipe a row of icing on the peak of the house where the two roof pieces will meet. Add the second roof piece. Pretty good-looking house already, isn't it?

Now comes the fun part (for kids of all ages). To decorate, just dab a bit of icing on each candy garnish and add to the house. Pipe in windows and doors.

A Gingerbread House of Your Own, continued

For roof: Shingles can be made using candy corn (a good buy if you go shopping right after Halloween), or M&M's, or any other such shape. For a thatched-roof effect, use shredded wheat.

Candy canes make wonderful decorations for the edges of the house—they hide unsightly seams! Just run a row of icing down the edges of the house and press the candy canes in place. The canes also make good door edges and window shutters.

Cooked Eggnog

12 large eggs

½ cup sugar

½ teaspoon salt

1 quart whole milk

2 pints half and half

2 teaspoons vanilla

nutmeg to taste

whipped cream for topping

6″ cinnamon sticks for garnish

In large saucepan, beat together the eggs, sugar, and salt. Whisk in 1 quart of milk. Cook over low heat, whisking constantly; do not allow the mixture to boil. Cook until the mixture thickens, just coating a metal spoon and running off slowly when you lift the spoon out of the mixture. (A thermometer should read 160° F. at this stage). Remove from heat and whisk in the half and half. Let mixture cool to room temperature, then refrigerate overnight or until it is thoroughly chilled. To serve, pour into individual glasses and top with a dollop of whipped cream, a sprinkle of nutmeg, and a cinnamon stick.

Chapter Thirteen

A German Christmas

Although I am only 25 percent German, I love German cooking 100 percent. And there is no better time for it than around the Christmas holidays. The smell of a pheasant or duck cooking in sweet cherry and port wine juices is special enough for any holiday tradition.

Spätzle is always a favorite, year round. But no one ever complains when you make it alongside a special dinner, too. If you have not yet succumbed to the lure of this deceptively simple food, you must try it, because all efforts to describe this dumpling fail to do it justice. The recipe included here makes quite a large batch, but you'll see why when you taste it.

And where would we be without making one or two batches of stollen for the holiday week? This deliciously rich bread is even called the Christmas loaf by many a cook. My recipe makes two loaves, which is more than enough for the Christmas Eve dinner, because you must have some for the next morning.

When I was just a young one, I learned that French toast made from stollen is the breakfast for Christmas Day. It was so good, it almost kept me from opening one or two presents before their time.

Roast Pheasant with Dressing

Spätzle

Stollen

Roast Pheasant

Serves 2 to 4

1 whole pheasant (or substitute duck or goose)

1 recipe dressing (recipe follows)

¼ cup port wine

¼ cup honey

1 tablespoon dried parsley, crushed

1 teaspoon dried savory, crushed

1 teaspoon dried thyme, crushed

Cut the pheasant into quarters and remove the larger bones from the thighs and breasts. (Your butcher can usually do this; it will make the eating of this delicious dish so much easier.) Lay the quarters out on a baking sheet and bake in a 350° F. oven for 45 minutes. Remove from oven; drain grease. Place a quarter of the dressing underneath each piece of pheasant, covering the dressing with the meat. Mix the port wine and honey together; add the parsley, savory, and thyme, and brush the mixture liberally on the pheasant. Return to oven and bake another 45 minutes, brushing every 15 minutes with the glazing mixture. Remove and keep warm until served. Serve each piece with the dressing.

Dressing

3 cups bread cubes, dried

¾ – 1 cup apple cider

½ cup fresh cherries, chopped

1 teaspoon dried parsley, crushed

1 teaspoon dried savory, crushed

1 teaspoon dried thyme, crushed

½ cup walnuts, chopped (optional)

Moisten the bread with the apple cider. Add all other ingredients and mix well.

Spätzle

Makes 6 cups

2 large eggs

1 cup lukewarm water

1 teaspoon salt

¼ teaspoon nutmeg

3 cups flour

2 tablespoons salad oil

2 tablespoons butter

1 tablespoon dried parsley, crushed

Beat the eggs into the water. Add salt, nutmeg, and flour to form a sticky, somewhat loose batter. To cook, bring a large pot of water to a boil. Add the *spätzle* batter to the water by pressing it through a colander or a *spätzle* cutter. Stir once to make sure the *spätzle* bits don't stick to the bottom. When they float to the top, they are done. Drain the *spätzle* and add the oil to them to prevent sticking together. When ready to serve, heat the butter in a frying pan. Add the parsley and *spätzle* and cook until they are hot. Serve immediately.

Stollen

½ cup warm water, 110° F.

2 packages active dry yeast

2 tablespoons sugar

1½ cups butter

additional ¾ cup sugar

3 eggs, beaten

1 teaspoon salt

1 cup warm milk

7½ cups flour

additional ½ cup flour

¾ cup raisins

¾ cup candied fruits, minced

1 cup almonds, chopped

additional ¼ cup butter, melted

½ cup brown sugar

1 teaspoon cinnamon

Egg Wash

1 egg

2 tablespoons water

In a small bowl, whisk the water and dry yeast with the 2 tablespoons sugar. Let this work until it is light and foamy. Meanwhile, in a large bread bowl, cream the butter and ¾ cup sugar. Add the eggs, salt, and warm milk. Mix together well. Add flour and stir. Turn dough out onto a floured counter and knead to form a smooth and elastic ball of dough. Cover the dough and let rise until doubled in bulk. Turn the dough out onto a floured counter again; flatten the dough slightly with the palms of your hands. Mix the raisins, fruits, and almonds together and sprinkle the additional ½ cup flour over this mixture to coat. Sprinkle a bit of this raisin mixture over the dough and work in by kneading. Continue to incorporate the mixture this way until all is worked into the dough. Divide dough in half. Roll out each half to an 8" by 15" oval. To the melted butter, add the brown sugar and cinnamon. Brush half the butter mixture onto each oval of dough. Roll the dough up into a loaf, sealing the seam underneath. Place each loaf on a cookie sheet and let rise until almost double in bulk.

Beat the egg with the 2 tablespoons of water to form an egg wash. Brush the top of each loaf with the wash and bake in a preheated 350° F. oven for 35 to 40 minutes.

Chapter Fourteen

The Ski Weekend

Winter is for skiing in our neck of the woods, which is Walworth County in the southeastern section of Wisconsin. The Kettle Moraine State Forest is less than two miles away (pretty close, when you're out in the country) and has hundreds of miles of trails. The trail systems are divided for hiking, biking, skiing, horseback riding, and snowmobiling. Cross-country skiers are in a winter paradise right in our own back yard. The trails are marked for both types of skiers, and there are various difficulty levels.

Additional trails are available at Old World Wisconsin, an outdoor living-history museum that reenacts life in the late 1800s.

With all that going for us, we get a lot of skiers. And skiers can work up a terrific appetite in just a few hours. That calls for good soup and hearty bread, two things we have in this menu.

Chicken soup is still a big favorite, but not many people make it from scratch any more. Well, they are missing out—there's only one way to achieve that smell wafting through the house.

And somehow, when most people think of vegetarian fare, all they can think of is a watery vegetable soup in a thin toma-

Chicken Soup with Kreplach

Brewery Black Bean Soup

Mom's Best Oatmeal Bread

Pumpkin Bread

to base. Our Brewery Black Bean soup is hearty enough to knock that idea right out of their heads.

Accompany these two great selections with Mom's Best Oatmeal Bread and a quick Pumpkin Bread, and you'll have them back on their skis in no time.

Chicken Soup With Kreplach

Serves 6–8

---

2 quarts chicken broth

1 recipe kreplach dough

1 recipe kreplach filling

To assemble, place 1 teaspoon of filling on each square. Brush 2 edges with water and fold over. Seal the edges with tines of a fork. Bring chicken broth to a boil and drop each kreplach into soup. Cover and cook for 10 minutes. Remove lid; turn heat to low if you need to hold the soup. Serve 4 kreplach to a bowl, with broth ladled over.

Chicken Broth

Makes 2 quarts broth

1 chicken carcass

1 ½ gallons water

1 Spanish onion

2 carrots

2 celery stalks

1 teaspoon dried marjoram, crushed

1 teaspoon dried thyme, crushed

1 tablespoon dried parsley, crushed

dash of cinnamon

salt to taste

white pepper to taste

In large stockpot, cover the chicken carcass with water. Wash the onion, but do not peel. Cut the onion in quarters and add to soup pot. Wash the carrots and celery, but do not peel, and add to soup pot. Add remaining ingredients and bring soup to a boil. Turn down to a slow simmer and cook uncovered for 1 ½ hours. Strain all solids from the broth and adjust seasoning with salt and pepper. Continue to simmer until stock is reduced to 2 quarts.

Chicken Soup With Kreplach, continued
Kreplach Dough
Makes about 24 kreplach

---

1 ½ cups flour

2 large eggs, room temperature,
   slightly beaten

dash of salt (optional)

lukewarm water

Place the flour in a bowl and make a well in the center. Add the eggs and salt. Add water a little at a time to form a stiff and compact ball of dough. This should be a very stiff dough, so don't add too much water. Turn out onto a floured counter and knead for 5 minutes or until dough is smooth and elastic. Cut dough into 2 portions. Roll out as thin as possible —⅛" to ¹⁄₁₆" thick. Cut into 4-inch squares.

Kreplach Filling

1 cup ricotta cheese

¼ cup sour cream

1 large egg, slightly beaten

1 tablespoon sugar

1 tablespoon fine, dry bread crumbs or
   matzo meal

2 tablespoons raisins, chopped, or currants

Combine all ingredients and mix well.

Brewery Black Bean Soup

Makes 10 cups

2 cups black beans

10 cups water

½ cup shredded carrots

½ cup shredded onions

1 can crushed tomatoes, 28-oz. size

3 tablespoons cider vinegar

1 teaspoon dried savory, crushed

1 tablespoon dried parsley, crushed

1 teaspoon dried thyme, crushed

1 tablespoon granulated garlic or
    1 teaspoon powdered

1 teaspoon black pepper

1 (12-oz.) bottle dark beer (Lowenbrau
    is good)

Place beans in stockpot and cover with water. Let soak overnight in the refrigerator. The next day, bring the beans and water to a boil over high heat; then turn down to a low simmer and add all remaining ingredients. Simmer for 2 hours, stirring occasionally. This is a very hardy vegetarian soup, but it easily accepts ham or sausage as an extra ingredient.

Mom's Best Oatmeal Bread
Makes 2 loaves

1 cup quick-cooking oatmeal

2 tablespoons butter

2 cups boiling water

½ cup warm water, 110° F.

2 tablespoons sugar

2 packages active dry yeast

2 eggs, beaten

½ cup molasses

2 teaspoons salt

6–7 cups bread flour

1 egg beaten with 1 tablespoon milk

2 additional tablespoons oats

Place oatmeal and butter in bread bowl. Pour in the 2 cups boiling water and stir. Let stand for 15 minutes. Meanwhile, in a smaller bowl mix together the ½ cup water, 2 tablespoons sugar and 2 packages yeast. Let the yeast work to form a puffy head of foam, then pour into the oatmeal mixture. Add the beaten eggs, molasses, and salt. Add 6 cups of the flour gradually while stirring to combine. Use the remaining flour to knead the bread. Let dough rise once, then form two loaves. Allow loaves to rise, then brush with the beaten egg mixture and sprinkle tops with the 2 tablespoons of oatmeal. Bake in preheated 325° F. oven for 30 to 35 minutes.

Pumpkin Bread

Makes 3 mini-loaves or 12 muffins

2 eggs

1 ½ cups sugar

1 cup prepared pumpkin

½ cup salad oil

¼ cup apple cider (or water)

¼ teaspoon baking powder

1 teaspoon baking soda

¾ teaspoon salt

½ teaspoon cloves

½ teaspoon cinnamon

1⅔ cups flour

½ cup raisins (optional)

½ cup chopped walnuts (optional)

In mixer bowl, beat eggs and sugar together. Add the pumpkin, oil, and cider and mix. Sift dry ingredients together and add gradually as you continue mixing. Add raisins and walnuts if desired. Pour into lightly greased and floured bread pans. Bake in preheated 350° F. oven for 35 to 40 minutes or until done. Muffins will take about 20 minutes.

Chapter Fifteen

Miscellany

Where would we be in life without this wonderful catch-all word? No matter what the rules, there are always exceptions. And so in this chapter you will find some of my most used herbal blends, sorethroat and cold deterrents, and treats for our critter friends.

The herbal blends can be adapted to anyone's household since they use dried herbs and may be stored for months if necessary. For me, they are an extension of the garden; many of the herbs listed grow quite well in our Wisconsin climate. Some readers may be interested in the savings offered by mixing their own blends. Surely you know someone who could benefit from the no-salt blend? And the Cajun or Italian seasoning may fit very nicely into your own or a friend's kitchen repertoire.

Natural cures are part and parcel of gardening tradition. You will find the horehound cough drops wonderfully soothing for sore throats, and horehound is easily grown from seed in little space. The cold deterrent I make I swear by. I simply don't have time to get sick, so the minute I feel a cold coming on, I whip up this concoction.

My garden also yields many a flower. The German in me says to use them to the best advantage. The Irish says yes, but

Herbal Blend for No-Salt Diets

Ragin' Cajun

Italian Seasoning

Horehound Cough Drops

Cold Deterrent

Candied Violets

Herbal Vinegars

Dog Gone Biscuits

A Cook's Favorite Bird Food Recipe

Replacement Formula

only in prettily pleasing dishes. Both requirements are met in the candied violets and herbal vinegars.

Finally, life would not be complete without the animals that share it with us. For those in the know, my little red barn is really "The Therapy Barn," a place to find comfort in the soulful eyes of a sheep, the playful curiosity of a goat, the empathy of a horse, or the industry of an old mother hen. So there are treats here for creatures as well.

My hope is that one or two of these offerings will strike a chord within your soul. If you find them all to be useful—well, we need to talk, soul mate.

Herbal Blend for No-Salt Diets

Makes 1 cup.

Excellent on poultry or pork

4 tablespoons dried marjoram, crushed

4 tablespoon dried thyme, crushed

5 tablespoons dried parsley, crushed

3 tablespoons dried sage, crushed

2 tablespoons garlic powder

2 tablespoons onion powder

1 teaspoon cinnamon

Blend together and store in tightly sealed container. A filled half-pint canning jar with a pretty ribbon makes a nice gift.

Ragin' Cajun

Makes 1 cup

6 tablespoons dried parsley, crushed

6 tablespoons dried thyme, crushed

2 tablespoons grated dried lemon zest

2 tablespoons dried red pepper flakes

1 tablespoon dried bay leaves, crushed

1 tablespoon black pepper

2 tablespoons dried basil, crushed

Blend together and store in tightly sealed container. May be used for "blackened" dishes or for jambalaya.

Italian Seasoning

Makes 1 cup

4 tablespoons dried parsley, crushed

4 tablespoons dried thyme, crushed

4 tablespoons dried oregano, crushed

3 tablespoons dried basil, crushed

1 tablespoon dried bay leaves, crushed

1 tablespoon white pepper

Blend together and store in tightly sealed container. Use for making Italian soups and tomato sauces and for seasoning meats. Please note that there is no garlic or onion listed here. I add those as fresh ingredients. If you prefer, add 4 tablespoons of the powdered variety of each to this recipe for a complete seasoning.

Horehound Cough Drops

Makes 12 dozen

1 cup crushed horehound leaves

1 ½ cups boiling water

1 ½ cups maple syrup

Pick the horehound in early morning when the oils provide the best flavor. Crush and place in bowl. Pour the boiling water over and let steep for 30 minutes. Strain out leaves and put liquid in saucepan with the maple syrup. Bring to a hard boil and continue boiling to hard-crack stage or 300° F. on a candy thermometer. Remove from heat and pour onto lightly buttered cookie sheet. Let cool slightly, then cut into 1" squares. When completely cool, separate squares and wrap in cellophane or waxed paper, twisting the ends.

Cold Deterrent

½ cup chamomile flowers

1 ½ cups boiling water

1 ½ cups apple cider vinegar

2 teaspoons ground cayenne pepper

½ teaspoon salt

3 tablespoons honey

Place chamomile flowers in pot and pour boiling water over. Let steep for 30 minutes, then strain, reserving the liquid. To the liquid, add cider vinegar, pepper, salt, and honey. Combine well and store in refrigerator. Take ½-cup dosages every 4 hours throughout the day, heating the mixture first.

ied Violets

3 pints *let flowers*

2½ cups sugar

2 cups water

Pick the violets in the early morning when they have just opened. Boil the sugar and water together to reach a temperature of 275° F. on a candy thermometer; remove from heat and pour into cookie sheet with sides. Place violets bottom-up in the sugar water. Let stand until they become somewhat translucent, then remove and place right-side-up on paper towel to dry. The violets may be stored between sheets of waxed paper in a dry location. Use them to garnish summer desserts of fruit or chocolate.

Herbal Vinegars

Herbal vinegars make wonderful hostess gifts, and they are so easy to make. But remember to package them prettily, too! Save your clear wine bottles and corks or use old bottles that may be clear or lightly colored. You can buy corks at a craft store or brewery supply house. Cork the bottles tightly and store. Use the herbal vinegars as a base for salad dressings, for marinating meats, for dashing across steamed vegetables, or for making a hot tea.

Just load your chosen bottle with a bunch of herbs or flowers and then add either white or cider vinegar. Here are some favorite combinations.

White vinegar with nasturtium blossoms,
> for a peppery taste with great color; good for salads.

White vinegar with peppermint or spearmint,
> for use in a digestive-aid tea.

Cider vinegar with chives,
> for a marinade for sauerbraten.

Cider vinegar with rosemary and tarragon,
> for chicken breasts cooked on the grill.

Cider vinegar with whole red chili peppers,
> for a dressing base for spicy pasta salads, hot or cold.

Dog Gone Biscuits

Makes 3 dozen 1" x 4" dog biscuits

1 cup whole wheat flour

½ cup cornmeal

¼ cup brewer's yeast (available at
  health-food stores)

½ cup bulgar wheat (available at health-
  food stores and some supermarkets)

2 tablespoons parsley flakes

1 teaspoon active dry yeast dissolved
  in ¼ cup warm water

½ cup milk

1 tablespoon chicken bouillon granules

1 beaten egg with 1 tablespoon water
  for glaze

Put yeast in the warm water and whisk to dissolve. When the yeast starts to foam, add the milk and chicken bouillon; stir to combine. In separate bowl, blend all dry ingredients. Add wet to dry, mixing with your hands till a dough forms. If the dough is a little stiff, add just a few more drops of water. Flour your counter liberally and roll out dough. Cut out with biscuit cookie cutter (I found mine at a hardware store), and transfer biscuits to cookie sheets. Brush each biscuit with the egg-and-water glaze. Bake at 250° F. for about 1 hour. Turn off oven and let biscuits dry overnight. Store in airtight container.

A Cook's Favorite Bird-Food Recipe

1 cup ground suet, melted or microwaved until softened

2 cups peanut butter, creamy or chunky

1 cup yellow cornmeal

½ cup whole wheat flour

1 cup leftover bread or muffin crumbs

½ cup ground nuts mixed with ½ cup raisins, dried cranberries, or currants

In blender, mix the suet and peanut butter. Turn out in bowl and mix in cornmeal, wheat flour, and crumbs. Form into four balls and roll in nuts and raisins. Hang in a net bag (an old onion or potato bag works well) or place in a suet rack on your bird feeder. May be stored in the refrigerator for one week (suet may become rancid after that) or frozen for future use.

Replacement Formula for Baby Animals

This has gotten me through many adoptions. Kittens and puppies thrive on this formula. But I've also used it for baby rabbits and pygmy goats in a pinch. There may be replacement formula available at your vet's, tailor-made for each species, but this recipe will get you through the times when you need it now.

4 egg yolks, beaten

¼ cup honey

2 cups goat's milk or whole milk from your refrigerator

2 teaspoons liquid children's vitamins (optional)

Beat the egg yolks until frothy. Add the honey and beat some more. Add the milk and liquid vitamins. Store, covered, in refrigerator for 3 or 4 days. Take out only what you need in one feeding, place in bottle or small glass, then set in a bowl of hot water to warm. Room temperature is good. Test the temperature before feeding. Use eyedropper or baby bottle. Call your vet for proper amounts and timing.

Index

A Cook's Favorite Bird-Food Recipe, 121

A Gingerbread House of Your Own, 92-95

Apple Butter, 8

Apple Cider Glaze, 64

Apple Jam, 78

APPLES

   Apple Butter, 8

   Apple Cider Glaze, 64

   Apple Jam, 78

   Apple Tart, 72

   Roman Apple Cake, 59

   Wild Rice Sauté, 23

Apple Tart, 72

Artichokes, Steamed, 15

Bacon Salad, Hot Spinach and, 62

Baked Brie with Garlic Crust, 13

Baked Custard, 66

BEEF

   Chuck Wagon Chili, 85

   Yankee Pot Roast, 37

Beer-Batter Fiddleheads, 22

BEVERAGES

   Chamomile-and-Mint Iced Tea, 34

   Cooked Eggnog, 96

Biscuits, Butter, 8

Black Bean Soup, Brewery, 107

Black Walnut Pie, 25

BLUEBERRIES

   Blueberry Blintzes, 42-43

Blueberry Pie Filling, 42

   in Garden Salad with Citrus Dressing, 29

Blueberry Blintzes, 42-43

Blueberry Pie Filling, 42

BREADS

   in Cranberry Bread Pudding, 9

   Freezer-Batter Zucchini Bread, 71

   Irish Soda Bread, 40

   Mom's Best Oatmeal Bread, 108

   Pumpkin Bread, 109

   Stollen, 101

   Whole Wheat Bread, 55

Brewery Black Bean Soup, 107

Broccoli and Ham Quiche, 30

Broiled Oysters on the Half Shell, 14

Butter Biscuits, 8

BUTTERMILK

   in Irish Soda Bread, 40

   in oatmeal pancakes, 7

   in Roman Apple Cake, 59

CABBAGE

   Cabbage Patch Soup, 69

   Crunchy Coleslaw, 48

Cabbage Patch Soup, 69

CAKES

   Chocolate Raspberry Cheesecake, 16

   Roman Apple Cake, 59

Candied Violets, 118

Caramelized Fruit over Baked Custard, 66

Chamomile-and-Mint Iced Tea, 34
CHEESE
  Baked Brie with Garlic Crust, 13
  in Broccoli and Ham Quiche, 30
  Green Eggs and Ham, 3
Cheesecake, Chocolate Raspberry, 16
Cherry Sauce, Cranberry, 77
CHICKEN
  Chicken Soup with Kreplach, 105-106
  Church Tent Fried Chicken, 84
  Homemade Chicken Salad, 56
Chicken Soup with Kreplach, 105-106
Chili, Chuck Wagon, 85
Chocolate Raspberry Cheesecake, 16
Chuck Wagon Chili, 85
Church Tent Fried Chicken, 84
Cinnamon Rolls, 83
Cocktail Sauce, 14
Cold Deterrent, 117
COLD REMEDIES
  Cold Deterrent, 117
  Horehound Cough Drops, 116
Cooked Eggnog, 96
COOKIES
  Fruit-Cake Gems, 90
  Gingerbread Cookie Cutouts, 89
  Rum Balls, 91
Country Scramble, 6
CRANBERRIES
  Cranberry Basting Sauce, 64
  Cranberry Bread Pudding, 9
  Cranberry Cherry Sauce, 77
  in Spring Greens with Raspberry
      Vinaigrette, 21
Cranberry Basting Sauce, 64

Cranberry Bread Pudding, 9
Cranberry Cherry Sauce, 77
CREAM CHEESE
  in Chocolate Raspberry Cheesecake, 16
  in Vegetarian Sandwich Filling, 57
Creme Fraîche, 43
Crêpes with Fresh Peaches, 4-5
Crunchy Coleslaw, 48

Dandelion Greens, 21
DESSERTS See also CAKES; PIES
  Apple Tart, 72
  Baked Custard, 66
  Blueberry Blintzes, 42-43
  Caramelized Fruit Over Baked Custard, 66
  Cinnamon Rolls, 83
  Cranberry Bread Pudding, 9
  Creme Fraîche, 43
  Gingerbread Dough, 92
  A Gingerbread House of Your Own, 92-95
  Icing (for A Gingerbread House of Your
      Own), 94
  Mocha Fudge Sauce, 51
  Rhubarb Torte, 33
  Stollen, 101
  Streusel Topping, 33; 59
  Sweet Tart Pastry Dough, 72
  Sweet Adelines Cream Puffs, 86
Dog Gone Biscuits, 120

EGGS
  in Baked Custard, 66
  Cooked Eggnog, 96

EGGS, continued
  in Country Scramble, 6
  Green Eggs and Ham, 3

Farmers' Market Salad, 70
FISH
  Pan-Fried Bluegills, 47
FLOWERS, EDIBLE
  Beer-Batter Fiddleheads, 22
  Candied Violets, 118
  Chamomile-and-Mint Iced Tea, 34
  in Cold Deterrent, 117
  Farmers' Market Salad, 70
  Lion-Naise Potatoes, 32
  in Spring Greens with Raspberry
    Vinaigrette, 21
Freezer-Batter Zucchini Bread, 71
FRUIT *See also* specific fruits
  Caramelized Fruit Over Baked Custard, 66
  Fruit-Cake Gems, 90
Fruit-Cake Gems, 90

Garden Salad with Citrus Dressing, 29
Garlic Crust, Baked Brie with, 13
Gingerbread Cookie Cutouts, 89
Gingerbread Dough, 92
Green Eggs and Ham, 3
Grilled Smoked Turkey Breast, 63

HAM
  Broccoli and Ham Quiche, 30
  Green Eggs and Ham, 3

Herbal Blend for No-Salt Diets, 113
Herbal Vinegars, 119
Homemade Chicken Salad, 56
Honey Butter, 15
Horehound Cough Drops, 116
Horseradish Sauce, 22
Hot Spinach and Bacon Salad, 62

ICE CREAM
  old-fashioned freezer, directions for, 50
  Old Fashioned Vanilla Ice Cream, 51
Iced Tea, Chamomile-and-Mint, 34
Icing (for A Gingerbread House of Your
  Own), 94
Irish Soda Bread, 40
Italian Seasoning, 115

Lion-Naise Potatoes, 32

Marinating Sauce, 65
Mint Iced Tea, Chamomile-and-, 34
Mocha Fudge Sauce, 51
Mom's Best Oatmeal Bread, 108
Morel Sauté, 24
MUSHROOMS
  in Country Scramble, 6
  Morel Sauté, 24
Mustard Greens, 21

Oatmeal Pancakes, 7
Orange Marmalade, 79

Oysters on the Half Shell, Broiled, 14

PANCAKES
   Oatmeal Pancakes, 7
   Potato Pancakes, 49
Pan-Fried Bluegills, 47
PASTA
   Farmers' Market Salad, 70
Peaches, Crêpes with Fresh, 4-5
Perfect Potato Salad, 58
PET FOODS
   A Cook's Favorite Bird-Food Recipe, 121
   Dog Gone Biscuits, 120
   Replacement Formula for Baby
      Animals, 122
Pierogi, 38-39
PIES
   Black Walnut Pie, 23
   Blueberry Pie Filling, 42
   "Simple as Pie" Crust, 23
POTATOES
   in Country Scramble, 6
   Lion-Naise Potatoes, 32
   Perfect Potato Salad, 58
   Potato Pancakes, 49
Potato Pancakes, 49
Pumpkin Bread, 109

Quiche, Broccoli and Ham, 30

Ragin' Cajun, 114

RASPBERRIES
   in Apple Tart, 72
   Chocolate Raspberry Cheesecake, 16
Replacement Formula for Baby Animals, 122
Rhubarb Torte, 33
Rice Sauté, Wild, 23
Roast Pheasant, 99
Roman Apple Cake, 59
Rum Balls, 91

SALADS
   Farmers' Market Salad, 70
   Garden Salad with Citrus Dressing, 29
   Homemade Chicken Salad, 56
   Hot Spinach and Bacon Salad, 62
   Perfect Potato Salad, 58
SAUCES
   Apple-Cider Glaze, 64
   Cocktail Sauce, 14
   Cranberry Basting Sauce, 64
   Cranberry Cherry Sauce, 77
   Creme Fraiche, 43
   Horseradish Sauce, 22
   Marinating Sauce, 65
   Mocha Fudge Sauce, 51
   Raspberry Vinaigrette, 21
   Strawberry Sauce, 75
   Tartar Sauce, 47
"Simple as Pie" Crust, 23
SOUPS
   Brewery Black Bean Soup, 107
   Cabbage Patch Soup, 69
   Chicken Soup with Kreplach, 105-106

Spätzle, 100
SPICES
　Herbal Blend for No-Salt Diets, 113
　Italian Seasoning, 115
　Ragin' Cajun, 114
SPINACH
　in Green Eggs and Ham, 3
　Hot Spinach and Bacon Salad, 62
SPREADS
　Apple Butter, 8
　Apple Jam, 78
　Honey Butter, 15
　Orange Marmalade, 79
　Sugarless Strawberry Jam, 76
Spring Greens with Raspberry Vinaigrette, 21
Steamed Artichokes, 15
Stollen, 101
STRAWBERRIES
　in Garden Salad with Citrus Dressing, 29
　Strawberry Sauce, 75
　Sugarless Strawberry Jam, 76
Strawberry Sauce, 75
Streusel Topping, 33; 59
Sugarless Strawberry Jam, 76
Sweet Adelines Cream Puffs, 86
Sweet Tart Pastry Dough, 72

Tartar Sauce, 47
Tortes, Rhubarb, 33
Turkey Breast, Grilled Smoked, 63

Vegetable Kabobs, 65

Vegetarian Sandwich Filling, 57
VENISON
　Wild Rice Sauté, 23
Vinegars, Herbal, 119

Walnut Pie, Black, 23
Watercress, 21
Whole Wheat Bread, 55
Wild Rice Sauté, 23

Yankee Pot Roast, 37

Zucchini
　Freezer-Batter Zucchini Bread, 71